THE CHRIST WE KNOW

HE CHRIST WE KNOW

JOHN BOOTY

Published in the United States of America by Cowley Publications.

International Standard Book No.: 0-936384-48-4.

The cover photograph, Graham Sutherland's *Crucifixion*, is reproduced by permission of the Vicar of St. Matthew's Church, Northampton, England.

Library of Congress Cataloging-in-Publication Data

Booty, John E.
  The Christ we know.

  Bibliography: p.
  1. Spiritual life--Anglican authors. 2. Spirituali
Anglican Communion. 3. Anglican Communion--Doctrines.
I. Title.
BV4501.2.B644 1987   248   87-6779
ISBN 0-936384-48-4

Cowley Publications
980 Memorial Drive
Cambridge, MA 02138

Acknowledgments

I wish to express my gratitude to the following for permission to reproduce works of art: St. Aidan's Church, East Acton, London for Graham Sutherland's *Crucifixion*; the Dean and Chapter of Llandaff Cathedral, Llandaff, Cardiff, Wales for Jacob Epstein's *Christ in Majesty*; the Dean and Chapter of Chichester Cathedral, Chichester, England for Graham Sutherland's *Noli me tangere*; S.P.A.D.E.M., Paris for Georges Rouault, *Obedient Unto Death, Even the Death of the Cross, Street of the Lonely, Christ in the Suburbs*, and *La Sainte Face* © S.P.A.D.E.M., Paris / V.A.G.A., New York, 1987.

"With Love from Judas," Edwin Brock, *Invisibility Is the Art of Survival* is copyright 1972 by Edwin Brock and reproduced by permission of New Directions Publishing Corporation.

"For the Time Being," W. H. Auden, *Collected Poems* is copyright 1945, 1975 by W. H. Auden and reproduced by permission of Random House.

I am also grateful for the invaluable assistance of Horton M. Davies, James Anderson, and Catherine Louise Booty in preparing this manuscript for publication.

CONTENTS

[vii]

Spirituality and Communion

What is spirituality? For some people it concerns what we do in church. For others it is identified with a personal devotion. Some dismiss spirituality as pious and individualistic, and irrelevant to the world's problems or the social responsibilities of Christians. There are those who confuse it with spiritualism and the attempt to make contact with the departed.

Perhaps the most damning understanding, or misunderstanding, associates spirituality with incense-clouded sanctuaries where pious Christians meet to be present at the reenactment of a sacred mystery and then go their ways, seemingly oblivious either to what they have experienced or what they might have experienced. Edwin Brock, in his poem, "With Love from Judas," wrote of one person who professed faith in the living Lord and yet failed to live that faith. The setting of the poem is

[1]

the breakfast table; the speaker has just come from early Mass.

> Christe eleison, the sweetest moment:
> dust motes in a shaft of sun and a setting
> by some simple soul; for a time
> the bruised knees are forgotten,
> clasped hands seem natural and
> a server's alb the only garment.
> And yet humility's the quickest of
> all failures, outside breathing
> the dust again. The breakfast table's
> our true setting: shrill our children's
> voices, taut their nerves.
> My daughter's manners are disgusting;
> my wife talks on of something trivial;
> the bacon's fat. Too soon the voice
> which whispered, 'Christ have mercy'
> is in my throat again. I watch tears
> run from my daughter's side, showing her
> no mercy. Repentance later will decide
> but, for this moment, Christ is dead.[1]

In actuality this man is more perceptive than most. As he shouts at his daughter and scorns his wife he is at least aware, most likely later on when his temper has cooled and he has had a chance to think, of what he has done and feels guilty. I would say that such a person is discovering what spirituality is all about. He is about ready to begin the journey, the spiritual journey, which is life — all of life — lived in the Spirit, the Holy Spirit communing with our human spirits. Any serious understanding of spirituality begins with a consideration of "spirit."

In the Book of Job, Elihu speaks of the spirit in human beings and identifies the spirit with "the breath of the Almighty" (32:8). Spirituality concerns the spirit, the breath, the life, the dynamic existence of the individual, without which no one could exist. Our initial focus, therefore, is not on something removed from day-to-day existence but on such existence itself, upon that which is ordinary. Hebrew-Christian faith identifies the necessary spirit of every person, ordinary and extraordinary, with God, God's dynamic presence amongst us and in us as his created beings. The human spirit is God's breath in us. God gives life, and the divine Spirit is that which animates us and, unless it be perverted or destroyed, gives us that understanding required for the achievement of the fullness of human existence, exemplified for us in God's Son, Jesus Christ. So spirituality is not divorced from rationality: it is the Spirit that makes us wise. Nor is Spirit divorced from the physical, for the Hebrew-Christian tradition acknowledges the interdependence of body and spirit. Spirit is involved in the entirety of human existence; it is concerned for wholeness.

This leads to a further daring assertion. God's Spirit, which the Bible speaks of as moving over the waters in the beginning of creation, dwells in every person, regardless of creed and even in the absence of creed. For God's Spirit is the divine, life-giving, dynamic Spirit without which no human being could exist. That this is not apparent to everyone points to the further fact that from the perspective of the Christian gospel, humanity is flawed. Multitudes of people endowed with life and thus with Spirit do not acknowledge the source of their lives, denying the relationship of the human spirit to its Creator-giver, blocking the ongoing work of God's Spirit to redeem the human spirit from its isolation in selfish preoccupation.

Although the Spirit is in every living, breathing person, the Old Testament in particular describes the Spirit descending upon charismatic leaders; it enables the prophets to be the voices of God in human history. In the New Testament we hear of the Spirit descending like a dove on Jesus at his baptism. We also have the narrative of Pentecost, where the Spirit's descent upon a people brings into being the church, which Paul refers to as the body of Christ. Furthermore, Anglican tradition teaches us that the Holy Spirit is given (some would say infused) to every baptized person. In that part of the initiation rite called confirmation, the bishop prays: "Almighty and everliving God, let your fatherly hand ever be over these your servants; let your Holy Spirit ever be with them; and so lead them in the knowledge and obedience of your Word, that they may serve you in this life, and dwell with you in the life to come. . . ." The Holy Spirit works with our spirits to lead us into the fullness of human existence as it was intended and begun with creation. It restores us to the image of God within us, causing spiritual growth and enabling us to live our lives in the Spirit, in obedience to God and his Word.

Who or what is the Holy Spirit? The Prayer Book catechism answers simply: "The Holy Spirit is the Third Person of the Trinity, God at work in the world and in the Church even now." Further on we read: "The Holy Spirit is revealed as the Lord who leads us into all truth and enables us to grow in the likeness of Christ." We recognize the Holy Spirit working in our lives as "we confess Jesus Christ as Lord and are brought into love and harmony with God, with ourselves, with our neighbors, and with all creation." Clearly, the church teaches us that the Spirit has to do with relationships, with God and with one another, and thus with sustaining love and harmony. Yet it is also clear that the catechism does not answer all of our questions, nor do its answers altogether satisfy the curiosity of modern inquirers. We find, as have many people down through the ages, that the Holy Spirit is elusive.

The Athanasian Creed, in the English translation, refers to the Holy Spirit as "incomprehensible." It does not mean that there is no possibility of understanding anything concerning the Holy Spirit, but rather that the Spirit cannot be fully encompassed or contained by human thought. This is true as well of the Father and the Son, but the particular elusiveness of the Holy Spirit is expressed in the thought that as soon as we believe that the Holy Spirit can be grasped intellectually, it disappears and we are confronted with Christ. This is so because the Spirit works to lead us to Christ. The Spirit is the activity of the Triune God found in "betweenness," that is, in the relationships which we experience that connect us or reconnect us to God, as God is made known to us in and through Jesus Christ. Much more will be said about the Holy Spirit in the pages that follow, but here, at the outset, we must acknowledge that the Holy Spirit, with whom "true spirituality" is concerned, exceeds our capacity to comprehend or fully understand.

The most appropriate response to God, Father, Son, and Holy Spirit, is not the modern quest for empirical or experiential proof; the proper response is adoration. It is only in the context of our adoration of the Triune God that we are inspired and enabled to understand with our hearts that which we can only imperfectly understand with our minds. In worshipping God the Holy Spirit, we abandon our defenses and open our hearts and minds to

[5]

receive that sacrificial love that arouses the responses of love toward God and toward all of God's creation. As we pray to the Trinity we gain wisdom, for we are engaged in the dynamic process at the heart of prayer - God breathing on us and into us, and we breathing, praying in response — prayer that is adoration and includes a deeper, fuller understanding of the divine mystery.

Spirituality, understood in terms of the God-given human spirit interacting with the redeeming Holy Spirit, is about communion. Spirituality concerns the human spirit going out, reaching out, transcending its isolated existence, in order to enter into relationship. At first it is with one other person, for the infant the all-important "mother." The relationship then extends to others, in family and beyond family in society, and ultimately with the wholly Other, the God from whom we come and toward whom we are journeying in both our individual and corporate histories. From the Christian perspective, it is not too much to say such reaching out by the human spirit is inspired by the Holy Spirit and that entering into relationship with another and with others finds its fulfillment when the individual, still in relationship to others, then enters into self-conscious relationship with God. As St. Augustine of Hippo said, addressing God at the beginning of his *Confessions*, "Thou awakest us to delight in Thy praise; for Thou hast made us for Thyself, and our hearts are restless, until they find their rest in Thee." George Herbert, the seventeenth century Anglican poet, expressed the same understanding when he wrote, "Life is straight,/ Straight as a line, and ever tends to thee." We may contest how straight the line may be for us in our personal experience, but the wisdom of Christians down through the ages agrees that involved in all of our reaching out there is a quest for God, that is, for that ultimate relationship which sustains and enriches all intermediate relationships.

Such an understanding of spirituality as communion emphasizes the wholeness of life, from birth to death and life eternal. As the new-born infant reaches out toward its mother, and thus acknowledges its dependence upon communion with another person, the child is beginning a life-long journey. That journey is enabled by the divine Spirit present at creation and bestowed anew at every critical turning-point along the way, until the growing person can say, with that faith that is itself the gift of the Spirit, "I believe."

As early Anglicans would put it, at baptism we are made righteous before God. Simultaneously, the Holy Spirit is infused in us. The Holy Spirit enters into communion with our marred spirits that we may have the power to grow in faith and love as we journey through life. Through baptism, that great cleansing sacrament of water and of energizing by the Holy Spirit, we are brought into the fellowship with other baptized persons in the church, which wholly depends upon the indwelling activity of the Holy Spirit binding person to person, as each is bound to God in Christ. The Spirit is given again and again in relationships with others, renewing the communion and being renewed in the communion that nurtures life.

Acknowledging that we were given the Spirit when we first breathed the breath of life and again when we were baptized, we pray, "Breathe on me, Breath of God," "Come down, O Love divine," "Come gracious Spirit, heavn'ly Dove,/ With light and comfort from above." The Holy Spirit is dynamic - the inspirer, enabler, sustainer of those relationships in life's journey that lead us to God and life eternal, in this present and beyond.

[7]

Spirituality and Communion

Spirituality on the Most Fundamental Level of Experience

Spirituality on the most fundamental level of human experience involves reaching out. Ultimately it is the individual in community reaching out toward communion with God. We first reach out, however, not specifically toward God, but toward other persons. We find ourselves transcending and going beyond ourselves into relationship with some other person and thereby into community with others. Community is born because the other we encounter is already engaged in relationships, most likely in entire, complex networks of relationships of varying degrees of seriousness and intimacy. We do not go out alone; we find the strength to venture on the basis of those first, life-giving relationships with our family that we experience after birth. Involving such activity, spirituality has to do with the necessary cultivation of the human spirit, the spirit that exists in intimate connection with the body. Such cultivation is essential if we are to mature as human beings, realizing our full potential and thus being what we were created to be.

Paul Tillich spoke of this reaching out toward others in terms of the necessary interaction of becoming an individual and of participation, subjects so basic that he dared to speak of them as "ontological elements," that is, elements concerned with being itself. He wrote of this dynamic in the context of his understanding of communion and of the realization of communion. "Communion," Tillich said, "is participation in another completely centered and completely individual self."[2] It was his conviction that no one exists without participation. No one can live — that is, no one can be recognized as possessing a consciousness-center personality — without belonging to some community. You cannot be an individual, a fully developed self, without entering into relationships where you run up against the reality of other people. It is in meeting this resistance that you discover self-identity and self-worth. Such resistance, however, is not a rejection but a meeting. It is the meeting of persons who do not seek to absorb one another and thus destroy one another, but rather seek to appreciate and enjoy one another, as they actually are and not as they may be imagined. It is in such encounter - mutual encounter - that we learn to know and to respect ourselves.

Such encounter is necessary. Unless checked by the resistance of others, the egotistical drive within each of us would result in our striving to dominate and then to conquer everyone whom we meet. Tillich states: "If he did not meet the resistance of other selves, every self would try to make himself absolute." It is also true that we take risks in reaching out to others. In that action we are vulnerable and we stand in danger of losing our personal integrity. Indeed, the consciousness-centered personality is in danger of dissolution in contemporary societies where the others whom we encounter denigrate our common humanity and use us or abuse us as things of no ultimate account or worth. The self that desires to be absolute is death to communion, such communion that is of any value to humanity. There is always, therefore, a moment of hesitation before each encounter, a testing period, when we seek to ascertain whether or not the person whom we are about to encounter respects us as individuals. There is something appropriate in those moments of anxiety when strangers encroach on our private space. How are we to know what their intentions may be? For any genuine encounter to occur, there must be risk and there will be anxiety until individuals meet and discover their mutual need and their respect for one another.

We dare not expect perfection in our relationships, however. We shall not always exist in a condition of mutual respect in any relationship. For one thing, we cannot always pick and choose our relationships in order to insure compatibility. We shall encounter people different from ourselves, different in terms of sexual identity, racial and ethnic identities, and social and educational backgrounds and assumptions. We shall know people whose commitments — religious, political, and others — differ from ours. There will be times when our differences overshadow our mutual appreciation and we shall need either to work on our relationships or to pass on to new ones. Then, too, there will be change. A relationship full of respect will turn sour, but on the basis of previous experience we can hope for a restoration of friendship. Indeed, it is important to realize that spirituality understood in terms of the communion of individuals, spirit with spirit, is never static but always dynamic. By its very nature, those relationships we identify with spirituality involve tension, sometimes painful and potentially destructive, but also full of promise. Even the most broken of friendships can become creative and fulfilling.

In our Western society there is a common assumption that tension is "bad," and that tensions are personally and socially destructive. Before stopping with such judgments we should consider the way in which the ancient Greeks taught that harmony proceeds from tension. The string in the lyre is held in tension by two opposing ends of the musical instrument. In order for the musician to pluck the string, creating an harmonious sound, *musicum carmen*, tension is a necessary condition. So it is in human relationships. There is a destructive form of tension, of course, but not all tension is destructive and indeed much tension is creative. The tension involved in the resistance of selves in communion with one another can be creative, enhancing individuals with a richness surpassing anything and everything that they possess.

True communion is not the sweet and simple mingling of kindred spirits. True communion involves the actual encounter of persons who must first recognize their individual distinctiveness, their challenging otherness. It is when this mutual recognition has occurred and the tension is acknowledged that persons can enter into communion, which is a union that respects the integrity of the individuals involved. The struggle of an adolescent with his parents is creative when the people involved can respect one another without falsifying either their relationship or the developing estrangement. The father assists the son in gaining a fuller, more complete sense of self and of self-worth. The son assists the father in discovering a peer and a friend where there was once a dependent child. In the process the relationship may seem disastrous, but in the end it can be a thing of beauty. This is the way it can be in any human relationship.

Furthermore, the kind of communion we have been exploring can illuminate our relationship to God. God is for us the wholly Other, who bids us to enter into a communion with him characterized not by warm feeling, but rather by creative tension. God accepts us as we are, finite and faulty; we yield to God in gratitude, but not without doubt and not without fault. The psalmist provides us illustrations, for at one time he will exclaim, displeased with his God,

> Awake, O Lord! why are you sleeping?
>> Arise! do not reject us for ever.
> Why have you hidden your face
>> and forgotten our affliction and oppression?

(Ps. 44:23-24)

But at another time he will express his deep satisfaction:

> God is our refuge and strength,
>> a very present help in trouble.
> Therefore we will not fear, though the earth
>> be moved,
>>> and though the mountains be toppled into
>>>> the depths of the sea;
> Though its waters rage and foam,
>> and though the mountains tremble at
>>> its tumult.
> The Lord of hosts is with us;
>> the God of Jacob is our stronghold.

(Ps. 46:1-4)

Whether displeased or satisfied, the psalmist lives in communion with his God. As they converse with one another the psalmist realizes the deepest truth about himself in his uneven but steadfast relationship with God.

Spirituality is Social

Contemporary Americans are notably religious, at least by comparison with people of other nations in the west, but their religion tends to be individualistic and private, anti-social and anti-institutional. Religion for us tends to be something to be worked out within the confines of our own lives, each of us bringing together, from the variety of stock-piles available, values and meanings that best serve our personal needs and fulfill our personal desires. It is not surprising to find that opinion polls reveal that a majority of Americans say they believe in God, but that only a minority attend a church or synagogue.

Building on the research of Robert Bellah, the sociologist of religion, Martin Marty concludes that in our century religion is apparently "diffused throughout the culture, difficult to grasp or observe. It has become a private affair, its fate no longer tied to organizations and institutions. Thus it has been only apparently paradoxical to observe that in the earlier generation religious institutions prospered while they shrouded a deeper secularization, yet in the second generation they languished while religion itself thrived."[3] We are here, of course, concerned with a major trend in the modern era. Individualism, over against the institutional and corporate, is an important value in Western culture. Yet when individualism runs rampant and serves selfish ends to the destruction of the welfare of others, it becomes demonic. A fact of the twentieth century is that, by comparison with Christianity and the other major world religions, the religion of many in our time is in fact destructive and demonic. Such religion is private and individualistic, virtually invisible, a matter of authenticating and bolstering life-styles that flatter our egos and provide for the satisfaction of our passing facies.

In spite of this privatized "religion," however, there persists another myth of American society. It is identified by James Oliver Robertson as the quest for

community. The English came to Roanoke, to James-
town, Plymouth and Salem, in order to create
communities. Ever since, attempts have been made with
varying degrees of success to achieve true communion.
True communion, so far as it can be identified in history,
is a symbiosis of individuality and community. Two
dissimilar organisms live together, to their mutual benefit,
in a dynamic relationshp full of tension and abounding
with hope. Never fully or satisfactorily realized, the
quest for communion in our society is never altogether
abandoned. Even in moments of the greatest selfishness
the value of communion is reasserted by those concerned
to preserve an American myth which we view as essential
to the well-being of our society.

Through our history the ideal of such communion is
found not in the urban megalopolis, but rather in the
rural and agrarian small town where individuality is cul-
tivated through mutual interdependence in a helping
community. As Robertson says:

> The necessity to create a community, in the midst of
> atomization, social vacuum, ignorance, self-doubt,
> and youth, is one of the most powerful, long-lasting,
> and painful of the imperatives of American myths.
> Individualization and community are bound together
> in agonizing symbiosis: the atomization which
> normally occurred in the process of migration, for
> example, brought with it the intense efforts of
> immigrants to create some kind of community — in
> Haight-Ashbury as on slave ships, on the frontier as
> in the cities.[4]

Robertson's observation is related to what I have said thus
far concerning spirituality. Viewed from a Christian per-

spective, spirituality is social. It involves the quest of all people, not merely Americans, for fulfillment in communion and thus for liberation from paralyzing isolation. Such an understanding issues in the refutation of all so-called spiritualities that concern individuals apart from the social contexts in which they live, and without which they would cease to exist. These social contexts stretch from the intimacy of the nuclear family to the larger communities of the city and the nation, and ultimately, in this twentieth century, to the global community, the entire people of planet earth.

An individualized spirituality is incomplete and its sought-after community is truncated until it encompasses all people and all times. This is so because the goal of the human spirit as it reaches out to communion with others ultimately issues in communion with the God in whom all people, places and times have their origins and their ends or purposes. The quest for communion is a quest that is always reaching out to include more and more of humanity and ultimately more of creation, human beings and nature alike, within its grasp. Such spirituality is no respecter of persons; it is not concerned with race or nationality or caste save for the ways in which distinctiveness adds to the beauty and creativity of the whole. This spirituality is universal. For those who call themselves Christians it is one with the universality of the gospel; for those in the traditional churches down through the ages it is represented by *episcopé* that is, by bishops and the gospel which they guard and proclam, passing it on from generation to generation.

Furthermore, such spirituality involves an attitude of universal acceptance. Archbishop Helder Camara exemplified spirituality as universality, the church through the episcopate as all-encompassing, when he said, "The bishop

[15]

belongs to all. Let no one be scandalized if I frequent those who are considered unworthy or sinful. Who is not a sinner? . . . Let no one be alarmed if I am seen with compromised and dangerous people, on the left or the right . . . Let no one bind me to a group . . . my door, my heart must be open to everyone, absolutely everyone."[5] The Christian gospel is universal and all-inclusive. In spite of the actions and attitudes of many Christians, faith in Christ is inclusive and not exclusive. Christian spirituality, therefore, does not reject out of hand the spiritualities of other faiths. Indeed, the minister of Christ recognizes that God is the source and the end of all, the alpha and the omega, that every genuine spirituality springs from the urge toward self-transcendence and thus toward liberating and fulfilling relationships with others. This does not mean that anything called "spirituality" is acceptable. The "spirits" must always be tested, because spirituality can be and often has been so corrupted that it becomes the purveyor of evil. For the Christian, the test consists in conformity to the life of Christ to whom the Holy Spirit bears witness. For example, the ideology of Hitler and the Aryan or master race is one that indeed concerned the quest for community, but it was for an exclusive and not a universal community. True spirituality can never issue in holocaust.

Christians also are ready to acknowlege that God works through other faiths. They can see that there are elements in differing faiths that tend toward the recognition of a common, although inwardly diverse spirituality and that the possibility exists for God to be working through other faiths to perfect the faith and thus the spirituality of Christians. In order to grasp what I am saying here it is important to realize that I have in mind the great established, world religions, with their varying strengths and weaknesses. If I claim a uniqueness for Christianity, it is in terms of its universality, its inclusiveness. Christ died for all people, "everyone, absolutely everyone."

Spirituality and Wholeness

Christianity concerns a communion that is universal and hence all-inclusive. Christian spirituality then concerns the recovery of wholeness in this broken world, in this time of specialization and fragmentation. The poet William Butler Yeats expressed this conviction in his poem, "Sailing to Byzantium":

Things fall apart, the centre cannot hold;
Mere anarchy is loosed upon the world,
The blood-dimmed tide is loosed, and everywhere
The ceremony of innocence is drowned;
The best lack all conviction, while the worst
Are full of passionate intensity.

In this latter part of the twentieth century there is much alarm at the growth of specialization and fragmentation in the social order as well as in the individual self. Where there was once a reasonable degree of order, we now have on the right, the disorder caused by unbridled competition of peoples striving for superiority and, on the left, the chaos caused by unworkable egalitarianism. In the middle of this, on the right and on the left, people are fragmented and tormented by the irresponsible activities of arrogant terrorists. In the face of this chaos, the individual self crumbles under the pressures of anxieties and fears, of stress and meaninglessness, and of the menacing reality of the "bomb."

David Bohm, an English theoretical physicist, views fragmentation as a kind of modern sickness. But he does more than lament this sickness. Bohm lays the blame for it on our unwarranted assumption that our human perceptions of reality are accurate. We actually think that our views about the world correspond with what we like to call "objective reality." It is understandable that in our preoccupation with distinctions and differences, day in and day out, we in time come to assume they are *actual* divisions. Thus the world of our experience is believed to be fragmented, consisting of nothing but atomized particles. To the contrary, says Bohm,

> what should be said is that wholeness is what is real, and that fragmentation is the response of this whole to man's action, guided by illusory perception, which is shaped by fragmentary thought. In other words, it is just because such reality is whole that man, with his fragmentary approach, will inevitably be answered with a correspondingly fragmentary response. So what is needed is for man to give attention to his habit of fragmentary thought, to be aware of it, and thus to bring it to an end. Man's approach to reality may then be whole, and so the response will be whole.[6]

It would not be wise to attempt a denial of this sickness and of its reality for modern people. The disorder, the anxiety and fear, are altogether too real to be dismissed as illusory. Those who live in the midst of disorder, anxiety, and fear know that they are not imagining their condition. What we must deny is our wrong-headed conclusion, based upon human experience of fragmentation, that what we perceive is reality itself. This tendency, in addition to falsifying reality, exacerbates the situation of disorder, anxiety and fear, plunging people into hopeless despair. The remedy for this condition, beyond a recognition of the "habit of fragmentary thought," would involve awareness of the interconnectedness and interdependence of all that is on planet earth, from atoms to nations.

Reality is whole. This is the testimony not only of Bohm and of other theoretical physicists, but also of Christian spirituality. Indeed, Christian faith perceives the interconnectedness and interdependence of all that is, in relation to God as creator, redeemer and sanctifier. It is the perception of all reality as originating with God, sustained by God, and being brought to completion by God that constitutes the major defense against disorder, anxiety and fear.

T. S. Eliot, along with the British idealist philosopher F. H. Bradley, whose works he studied, seemingly believed, contrary to the empiricist perception of reality in fragments, that reality is whole, an "unanalyzable whole." We think and act as if reality were a jig-saw puzzle, consisting of discrete, analyzable fragments, but it is more like a work of art which to be understood must be perceived as a whole, a unified subject-object. We tend as inhabitants of earth to comprehend ourselves in narrow terms, as Americans, and as particular kinds of Americans, identified in terms of gender, social class, race, political party, and so on and on. Reality is distorted by such perceptions of ourselves. The same tendency is rampant in the church, where members identify reality within the narrow confines of immediate experience. We analyze the church as composed of congregations, identified with particular buildings, composed of parish groups, sharing special interests and divisive prejudices. If the sociologists of religion are correct, we analyze religion in America into individuals, separately seeking self improvement and the alleviation of anxiety and pain. The fruits of our analysis we call "reality," but for the poet, and Christian spirituality, there is another reality, reality which sees things whole, interconnected and interdependent and identifies the planet earth with its Creator and the church with the Redeemer. The church as it is, prior to analysis into fragments, is an organic whole. The church is the body of Christ, a fellowship in the love of God whose mission is reconciliation. Such reconciliation is the restoration of an awareness in faith of the interconnectedness and interdependence of all Christians, as members of the one body in earth and in heaven, past, present, and future, of which Christ is the head.

How do we know that reality is whole if, as soon as we apprehend it, we analyze it, divide it into pieces, and view it in fragments? F. H. Bradley's answer would be that we know it by a process prior to thought, that is by "immediate experience," feeling without object or subject (akin to the unified sensibility of the metaphysical poets of seventeenth century England: Donne and Herbert and Vaughan). It is encountered in a moment of intense awareness as a sensitive person encounters a revelation of beauty in a sublime work of art. It is the experience of the worshipper who in awe is encountered by a revelation of God (Eliot spoke of "annunciations" in word, in music, in the drama of the liturgy). The analysis of the immediate experience that follows such encounter tends to destroy it. The moment passes, and so too the awareness of the reality. This understanding of reality as whole perceived in immediate experience permeates Eliot's *Four Quartets*. But in his poetry Eliot does not express reality in its wholeness; it cannot be done for words crumble under the effort. He rather points to it, as R. L. Brett says, "by bringing us to those places and those experiences where the truth becomes manifest, beyond words. Truth for him, as for Bradley, is a matter of coherence, of seeing in human history and experience a pattern of significance. . . . "[7]

What is true of Eliot's poetry can also be considered as true of spirituality. Christian spirituality presupposes that reality is whole: it comes from, is sustained by, and ends with God. Spirituality involves the manifold forms of worship, places, and experiences where the truth becomes manifest; it takes hold of the faithful before we can grasp it and analyze it, as we instinctively seek to do. Spirituality involves seeing and understanding all that is in accordance with a pattern of significance, which we name "divine revelation." For those who engage in this spirituality, truth is "a matter of coherence and thus of seeing in human history and experience a pattern of significance," which God through the Holy Spirit makes known to us.

There is a further consideration. Andrew Louth, an English scholar at Oxford, takes seriously T. S. Eliot's widely-debated concept of the dissociation of sensibility - the loss of the association of thought and feeling in poetry - which he dates about the time of Dryden and Milton. "A thought to Donne," writes Eliot, "was an experience; it modified his sensibility." After the metaphysical poets, that is, after Donne, Herbert, and Vaughan, this habit of dissociation set in. It began with a refinement of language, together with a progressive crudeness of feeling, and later a sentimental revolt "against the ratiocinative" in the eighteenth century. Since then, poets have "thought and felt by fits, unbalanced." It is not my intention to pronounce on Eliot's theory here, but to pursue Louth's consequent thought, where he links dissociation with fragmentation and asserts that the two have afflicted and crippled not only Christians, but the entire theological enterprise in our time. Louth writes,

> One way in which the division [fragmentation] of theology manifests itself is in the division between theology and spirituality, the division between thought about God and the movement of the heart towards God. It is a division of mind and heart, recalling Eliot's 'dissociation of sensibility,' and a division which is particularly damaging in theology, for it threatens in a fundamental way the whole fabric of theology in both its spiritual and intellectual aspects.[8]

Theology for the Greek Fathers of the early church meant what we mean when we speak of both theology *and* spirituality. The Cappadocians, whose understanding of theology was centered upon the doctrine of the Trinity, believed that the discipline of theology involved a loving contemplation of the Trinity, an act that we now identify with spirituality. As Louth points out, theology for Evagrius of Pontus *was* contemplation. For Evagrius, a theologian "is one who has attained the state of true prayer: 'If you are a theologian, you pray truly, and if you pray truly, you are a theologian.'" Such is the eastern understanding in contrast to the western; with the latter, theologians are very often specialists who need not have any acquaintance with prayer or belong to any church.

In so many ways it is apparent that spirituality concerns wholeness and is itself inclusive. Spirituality is concerned with the whole of life, individual and corporate, secular and sacred, profane and mystical, from the cradle to the grave and from prehistory to the eschaton. Spirituality concerns all of our humanity, the mutual participation not only of ourselves with God in Christ, and of ourselves with one another in Christ, but of heart and mind, thought and feeling, a mutuality that T. S. Eliot called "unified sensibility."

It is our habit of viewing reality in fragments that causes us to speak of spirituality as though it were a discrete and separate entity. We see it as existing apart from theology, to which it essentially belongs, as well as from all those intersecting, interrelated modes of being, thinking, and feeling that constitute a human life and human community, and are intimately involved in spirituality. We should note here that the word "spirituality" in its most positive sense is modern, with roots in French Roman Catholicism. Yet for many people in our time it is a word standing "for those attitudes, beliefs, practices which animate people's lives and help them to reach out towards super-sensible realities," and based upon the assumption that spirit and body are altogether distinct and different.[9] Such an assumption runs contrary to the teachings of the Christian gospel and is akin to Gnostic and Manichaean heresies. For many people the word "spirituality" stands for the life of prayer, both personal and corporate, which is peculiar to historic Christianity and includes such disciplines as the practice of prayer. For others, "spirituality" has no peculiarly Christian meaning, but is used in relation to the "spirit" or "ethos" of some thing or of a group. Thus it can be used of those who attempt to manipulate or control persons or groups to their own benefit, or to advance their own special interests. The Neo-Nazis in America are an example of this.

Spirituality and Availability

In order to perceive reality as whole we need, as Bohm says, to be aware of our "habit of fragmentary thought," to be aware of it and to bring it to an end. The awareness of our distortion of reality as whole, and of the fragmentation of that wholeness as false and potentially evil, involves another and more routine habit. We must develop the habit of perceiving the jigsaw puzzle as a whole, its pieces integrally related, before we examine its parts one by one. This awareness of reality concerns seeing the all-inclusive pattern of reality as created and sustained by God, rather than imposing our own fragmented patterns on reality and thus, at least for ourselves, destroying the essential unity. It means perceiving the other not in terms of our needs and desires, or our fears - certainly not in terms of our selfish will to conquer the other - but rather as genuinely other with such substance and integrity so that we enter into lively communion with the other.

We may think here of the communion of lovers, where there is a communication of extraordinarily creative power as each views the other not only as they are, but as they can be, in a life-giving and life-enhancing relationship. I am reminded of Sonia, in Dostoevsky's *Crime and Punishment*. Sonia perceives Roskolnikov, the man who murdered her friend Lizaveta, with an awareness that overrides her pain and anger. What she sees in the murderer is the presence of suffering, and when he confesses his crime to her, Sonia does not flee in fear but rather turns to him and speaks these words: "What have you done to yourself? . . . Go at once, this very minute, stand at the cross-roads, bow down, first kiss the earth, which you have defiled, and then bow down to the whole world and say to all men aloud, 'I am a murderer!' Then God will send you life again." And she reminds him of Lazarus and speaks to him of hope and resurrection.

I also think of the painter Charlotte Salomon, the young Jewish woman who was destined to die in one of Hitler's death camps. During the time she was released from one concentration camp and waiting to be sent to another, Charlotte painted a picture of herself looking out of a window at God's good earth. Beneath the picture she wrote, "*Got mein Got, O ist das shon!* God my God, how beautiful it is!" In the presence of intense ugliness and despicable evil, she perceived the truth of the reality beyond it in spite of all evidence to the contrary. She was the victor, although she died at the hands of men who claimed the victory.

The French Catholic existentialist, Gabriel Marcel, distinguished between the spectator and the participant in the way both look at reality. The spectator standing before the Venus de Milo in the Louvre, sees the statue and considers the sculptor's skill, identifying the exact nature of the medium and the techniques used. His is the expert's appreciation of a great work of art. But it leaves him virtually untouched as he turns away to regard another art object. The participant, however, views the same statue, seeing it as a whole, without detailed analysis, and with a feeling of awe she enters into communion with it. What occurs is a communication between viewer and statue, communication whose origin comes at least in part from beyond the viewer. The participant departs

[25]

forever affected by what she has seen, her life challenged and enriched.

Sonia, Charlotte, and the woman at the Louvre all possess keen powers of awareness. Their awareness involves *accessibility* - the power to be open to communion and communication beyond ordinary experience, although it is not to be excluded from ordinary experience. Indeed, the awareness of which I speak is known to ordinary mortals in and through daily experiences, as the sudden awareness of spring's first flower, or the dawning awareness of the love that someone has for us, seemingly undeserved, quite irrational; or the awareness that comes in the moment when a diffucult, seemingly impossible problem is understood and a reasonable solution is apparent. It can be an awareness of another person's pain, a realization that elicits a response both sympathetic and helpful, that commits us to action on behalf of the suffering of others. Such was the awareness of the Good Samaritan, the awareness of Jesus as he encountered the physically and spiritually distressed.

The awareness and communication exhibited by Sonia, Charlotte, and the woman at the Louvre have been equated by Marcel with *disponibilité*, or "availability." In each case the individual has been open to another and has therefore been capable of giving in return. We know from the New Testament that it is better to give than to receive, but we cannot truly give until we have first learned to receive. The person able to receive is open to the other and to others and not only perceives and understands but is available in a relationship of giving and receiving. Further on in this chapter we shall observe an exceptional degree of availability in Jesus, as he received the Holy Spirit in baptism, called his disciples to follow him, and taught and healed.

What is the character of this availability? First, it should be noted that it has more to do with relationship than with moral goodness or wisdom. To be unavailable is to be cut off from mutual relationships with other people and with God. To be unavailable is to be enclosed in the fortress of the self. It is to withhold oneself from engagement with others. It is to be infected with *hubris*, or pride, and thus to behave as though the relationships we have are tentative and conditional. To be unavailable is to be as a captive, unable to receive and thus unable to give. Consider the husband who would like but is seemingly unable to commit himself to a receiving and giving relationship with his wife, and who thus watches as something most precious decays and dies. Consider the woman who cannot receive a gift without feeling it necessary to give in return, thus to be free from any personal indebtedness. The mental hopitals are populated with frozen, imprisoned selves. There we often find that unavailability in terms of self-preoccupation involves self-recrimination, whereby the sufferer is preoccupied with his own faults.

Gabriel Marcel understood the tragedy of self imprisonment and wrote: "The spirit of prayer, above all, is a welcoming (*accueillante*) disposition toward everything which can tear me away from myself, from my propensity to become hypnotized by my own faults."[10] The spirit of prayer is here understood in terms of availability, a breaking down of the walls of pride that imprison the self. To pray is to turn to God with an open spirit and to enter into a relationship of receiving and giving in which we are free to love and to be loved. The spirit of prayer has to do with turning, turning from

[27]

self, open to others and to God. This turning is what Christians have in mind when they speak of repentance, for in repentance the Christian turns to God in remorse for a marred and broken life and receives forgiveness, forgiveness such as enables thanksgiving, the forgiveness of others and life lived in service to our neighbors. Repentance, thus, has more to do with relationships than with sins, for sins have consequences and result in broken relationships, a turning away from God and others, ultimately to our own destruction. In order to perceive reality as whole, therefore, it is needful that we be available to that reality as revealed to us in God. Spirituality presupposes an openness to God and others.

Spirituality and the Gospel

Christian spirituality concerns the personal action of God, who enables the spiritual quest in which all people are involved by virtue of being human. We acknowledge the reality and necessity of self-transcendence, of going out into relationship with others. We see the importance of resisting the habit of fragmentary thought instead of seeing things whole, and of being available. In this quest we are inhibited by our bondage to the self, and to that closed state of being whereby we are spectators rather than participants, resisting the communion and communication essential to our well-being. We identify the personal action of God with the activity of the Holy Spirit in and among us, in community, through Word and Sacrament, in and through lives of prayer. The spirituality of the Christian has to do with the human quest as informed and empowered by God's intervening and enlivening Spirit.

[28]

In the familiar gospel account in Mark (1:10-11) of the baptism of Jesus, we read how Jesus was baptized by John in the River Jordan. When Jesus "came up out of the water, immediately he saw the heavens opened and the Spirit descending upon him like a dove; and a voice came from heaven, 'Thou art my beloved Son; with thee I am well pleased.'" Peter seemingly had this in mind when, after Jesus' death and resurrection, and after the coming of the Holy Spirit at Pentecost, he preached, saying, "God anointed Jesus of Nazareth with the Holy Spirit and with power . . . [and] he went about doing good and healing" (Acts 10:38). As John Taylor writes, for Jesus "the descent of the dove was a moment of seeing and hearing, in which he realized in a deeper, clearer recognition, his own role both as Son of God and as Suffering Servant."[11] The Spirit was upon him and, after being driven into the wilderness to wrestle with the meaning of this new ability to see and hear, he was ready to begin his ministry and mission, equipped with a power from beyond that marked him out as an altogether exceptional human being, the chosen of the Lord of Hosts.

Jesus as perfect man saw the extraordinary in the ordinary. He saw not only what was happening as he was baptized in the Jordan River, which anyone and everyone might see; he saw much more. Jesus saw the heavens opened, the clouds divided and the sky cloven in two. Through the cloven sky he saw the Spirit of God descending gently like a dove descending from the sky to light upon a tree, the Spirit lighting upon him, entering into him, body, mind, and spirit, endowing him with extraordinary powers of perception, awareness and availability, communion and communication.

We can see, after his baptism and after his temptation in the wilderness, how this power worked. Mark tells us that Jesus looked at certain ordinary fishermen, Simon and Andrew (Mk. 1:16), James and John (1:19), and at Levi, the tax collector, whom we know as Matthew (2:14). He looked and he saw not only what anyone might see — ordinary folk, common fishermen, a despised tax collector. He saw with strengthened and heightened perception, his senses tuned by the Holy Spirit to perceive fragments in relation to the whole and to understand beyond human understanding. Jesus saw what these men might become, the potential hidden from other eyes, and he beckoned them, calling them to follow him, to be his disciples and to be the beginning of a fellowship that would become the church, his body, the salt of the earth.

The Gospel of John (1:35-42) contains a theological interpretation of the calling of the first disciples. Two of them, one of whom was Andrew, had heard John the Baptist say of Jesus, "Behold, the Lamb of God!" They heard and they followed Jesus. Sensing their presence following him, Jesus turned to them and asked, "What are you looking for?" Here the gospel writer recognizes that Jesus *sees* them and, in asking what they are *looking for*, seems to be both asking them and empowering them to see that their need for liberation from the bondage of temporality, change, decay and death is now met in and through the one whom John called, "The Lamb of God." The disciples answer, "Rabbi, where are you staying?" This is a strange response and yet explicable when considered from the gospel's standpoint. They are asking, "Rabbi, where are you staying, where do you dwell, show us where you abide that we may stay, dwell, abide with you and thus abiding with you, in you may escape from bondage." Jesus answers, "Come and see." Raymond Brown reminds us that "coming" and "seeing" are words used subsequently in the Fourth Gospel to describe faith:

"It is interesting that in v. 40, vi. 40, 47, eternal life is promised respectively to those who believe in him — three different ways of describing the same action."[12] The Evangelist comments, "They came and saw where he was staying, and they stayed with him." The disciples followed Jesus and saw him with a degree of perception that was extraordinary, a vision that involved believing in the one they saw. Thus believing, they abided with him, which means in the light of the Greek word *menein* (to abide) used here and in John 6, they *participated* in him. He was in them and they were in him and, by virtue of this communion, the apostles were made new. They became inheritors of eternal life, liberated from the bondage of death, sin, and meaninglessness.

This is not the end of the evidence. In Mark, we find that the power of the Spirit led Jesus to see the faith of those who brought the paralytic to him for healing (2:5). He observed their faith, but he also was able to see unfaith, and thus Mark tells us of how some of the scribes who watched the healing of the paralytic doubted within themselves. In the story of Zacchaeus (Lk. 19) we have a despised tax collector, both rich and privileged, climbing a tree in order to see Jesus as he passed through Jericho. As he passed, Jesus looked up and saw Zacchaeus and informed him that he would stay at his house, knowing well that people would deride him for associating with a sinner. This knowledge did not stop Jesus, who perceived that Zacchaeus was ready to change his life as the Spirit worked to change him, to pledge to give one half of his goods to the poor and to restore fourfold to any he had defrauded. Zacchaeus acted out his repentance and Jesus proclaimed that salvation had come to his house.

In the story of the two blind men (Mt. 9:27-31) Jesus

asked, when they came to him, whether they believed that he was able to heal them. They responded by saying they did so believe. "Then he touched their eyes, saying, 'According to your faith be it done to you.' And their eyes were opened." Seeing and believing are here causally related. They believe and they see. Doubting Thomas (John 20) must first see, and touch, and then he would believe, but the point is made that for others, for all sceptics down through the ages, there must first be belief and then believing they would see with a perception beyond ordinary perception. They would see with the eyes of faith, eyes illumined by the Spirit of God to see and feel that which is beyond ordinary knowing.

And indeed there is feeling, as we note from the story of the woman with the issue of blood (Mk. 5:25-34). This woman touched Jesus' garment without his seeing her do it and her hemorrhage stopped, "and she felt in her body that she was healed of her disease. Jesus, perceiving in himself that power had gone forth from him, immediately turned about in the crowd, and said, 'Who touched my garments?'" His disciples wondered at his question. It could have been anyone. It was of no consequence. But Jesus knew otherwise and looked about himself to see who had touched his garment. Before he could discern her the woman came forward "in fear and trembling and fell down before him and told the whole truth. And he said to her, 'Daughter, your faith has made you well; go in peace, and be healed of your disease.'"

In addition, we have evidence of how Jesus came, through events of great significance to him if not to others, to a fuller awareness of his own mission. There is the example of the Syro-Phoenician woman (Mk. 7:24-30). She was a pagan from outside the house of Israel and thus beyond saving, according to common understanding. She wished him to cast out the demon that was afflicting her daughter and Jesus gave her his answer, "Let the children first be fed, for it is not right to take the children's bread and throw it to the dogs." In this way he indicated that his mission was restricted to the Israelites. But she, in an indomitably positive and optimistic way, countered him, "Yes, Lord; yet even the dogs under the table eat the children's crumbs." At that moment he perceived her faith, and also realized that his calling was far greater than he had previously understood it to be. It was to be to all people, beginning with the house of Israel. Jesus perceived in a moment that this pagan woman's faith was greater than any he had seen in Israel. Christian spirituality involves a heightened perception not only for ministering to those in need, but also as an aid to that spiritual growth which is the work of the Holy Spirit in us.

Christian spirituality is a matter of growing toward some end or purpose. That purpose has been revealed to believers in Jesus Christ, particularly through the ways in which he emphasized, in teaching and in living and dying, that the way of salvation is the way of servanthood and sacrifice. Our heightened awareness, our ability to see the extraordinary in the ordinary, is not given to please us and to make us feel superior. To the contrary, we are empowered to see and hear and feel so keenly in order that we may better serve people in their real needs, perceiving when and how to exercise the ministry of pardon, liberation, and healing.

We are accepted and loved by God not because we have deserved or earned God's approval, but because it is God's nature to love all that he has made and in particular those made in his image, the people of planet earth.

We know how much God loves because he gave his Son to die upon the cross in demonstration of his love and to unloose the great power of love that overcomes death and sin and meaninglessness. We are accepted, just as we are. We are forgiven sinners, because receiving that love we are sorrowful and plead with God for strength to be wholly given over to sacrificial service, to be instruments of the divine love for the salvation of others and for the redemption of the created order. We would be like our Lord, he who came among us not as a gentile king, but as a menial servant, revealing thereby that the true greatness toward which all humankind tends is not that of wealth and power but rather that of the servant who binds up the wounds of the maimed and shattered, pardons the sins of those who do evil, holds the suffering in his arms, comforting them, and in the end gives up his life for the sake of another.

We are accepted and at the same time endowed with God's Holy Spirit, that we may go the admittedly meandering way toward perfection, that is, toward wholeness. From the moment of our acceptance we have confidence that we dwell in, abide in, participate in Christ as he, through the on-going activity of his Holy Spirit working in consort with our spirits, dwells in, abides in, participates in us. So we are summoned into ministry, Christ's mission and ministry, serving the servant Lord as we serve the needs of others in his name, abiding more and more in our Lord as he abides in us.

Spirituality for Christians is following Jesus as his disciples, becoming his instruments for ministry and mission in and for the world - all people and all creation. Few people have wrestled with the meaning of discipleship more than Karl Barth. In his *Church Dogmatics* he emphasizes that the command to follow Jesus "is identical with the command to believe in Him." It requires that human beings, "should put their trust in God as the God who is faithful to the unfaithful." This is all that we have to offer, faith which is expressed in trust, but it is sufficient. Through the call of Jesus and the obedient response of Christians "solid ground is placed under [our] feet when [we are] on the point of falling into the abyss."[13]

The disciple is therefore the person who lives by trust in God. That this trust is not simple, and at times is infinitely difficult, is confirmed by countless numbers of witnesses through the ages. For example, the theologian John Skinner attests:

> Jesus says: Come with me. Follow me. To follow Jesus is to undertake an adventure into the unknown; it is to engage in risks which offer themselves as possibilities for existence. In following Jesus the future is ever before us in the symbol of a Cross. It is a symbol which judges us and also sets us free. The Cross is the possibility for the disciple's life in Christ. It becomes the disciple's future, the disciple's liberation, even the disciple's sanctification.[14]

Discipleship does not free us from tension and conflict. "Following Jesus," says Skinner, "involves the disciple in the complex issues which emerge from the fundamental tension between structure and spirit. Such tension must be maintained at all costs because it corresponds to the spiritual dynamic implicit in the condition for discipleship."

Because discipleship involves risks and does not free us from tension, and because being a Christian is fundamentally social, Christian discipleship involves the cultivation of that spirituality which increases the disciple's participation in the community of the faithful. It is within the church that the Christian receives support, and experiences the tension between a structured faith and the freedom of the spirit, and is thus empowered to live after the pattern of the servant Lord amidst the complexities and ambiguities of the society to which we belong.

Anglican Spirituality

Discipleship concerns the objective, formal worship of the people of God, both word and sacrament. It is the conviction of Anglicans that Christian spirituality is rooted in and arises out of the common prayer of the people who, brought together into relationship by the Holy Spirit, constitute the living body of Christ, continuing his mission and ministry through history. Anglican spirituality is not unique in its emphasis upon communion and community. It is also true of the tradition shared by all of the historic churches that trace their development from earliest Christianity. We come closer to something unique when we proceed to assert that Anglican spirituality is rooted and grounded in that which is identified as central to its emphasis on communion and community, and to the tradition called "Anglican": "the ongoing corporate, liturgical life of the Church" in which all people participate and which is focused on the *Book of Common Prayer*. Harvey Guthrie is right to say that

> Anglican spirituality arises out of the common prayer of a body of Christians who are united in their participation — through physical presence and liturgical dialogue and sacramental action — in the cult in

which the Church identifies itself as Church. It involves a corporate life whose times and seasons and ordinances and readings and sermons are the means of corporate participation, in and through Christ with God present to and for human beings in history in this world. Private devotion and prayer and meditation on the part of individuals are supports and means of putting oneself into and extensions of the ongoing, corporate, liturgical life of the Church.[15]

To put it another way, worship according to the *Book of Common Prayer* is a primary means whereby Anglicans encounter and are encountered by the Holy Spirit. They are fed, renewed, and brought into life-giving, saving relationships with one another, beginning in the pew and at the altar and extending into all of life.

It is not that Anglicans worship the *Book of Common Prayer*, but rather that they regard it as a holy instrument. The Prayer Book conveys through the rich interplay of Scripture and liturgy the saving drama which enables worshippers to enter into life-giving relationship with God in Christ by the activity of the Holy Spirit. This conviction concerning corporate worship, Scripture and liturgy, rests in part on the witness of Scripture itself and in part upon the example of the early church. It is a conviction confirmed by reason and experience.

Scholars who study closely the development of formal liturgies in the first centuries of the church's history have taught us that liturgy is essentially drama. Enlivened by the Holy Spirit, liturgy has a powerful effect on us as we participate in its action, drawing those open to the Spirit's working into communion with God and with one another as we meet in fellowship (*koinonia*) with God. Word and sacrament are both involved, but I would rather speak of the divine drama, the saving action of the liturgy - liturgy that consists of word, sacrament, Spirit, and people. Thus it is not the Prayer Book itself that is central, but the script (or scripts) of the sacred drama contained in it. What is most essential is the drama, performed by people who enter into it wholly, open to its manifold effects, directed and enlivened by God's Holy Spirit.

The key word is "communion," by which Anglicans sometimes mean the reception of the consecrated bread and wine, the body and blood of Christ, and sometimes the Holy Communion, the entire sacrament. Influenced by the fathers of the early church, particularly the Cappadocians, Richard Hooker stressed the importance of the concept of "communion" for an understanding of the Prayer Book and of Christian worship in general. He interpreted the essence of the sacrament of the Holy Communion in terms of participation and of mutual participation. By participation or communion he meant not only *koinonia* (1 Cor. 10:16) or fellowship, a mutual relationship with its emphasis on giving and receiving, but also *menō (menein)*, meaning to abide in or be in union with. In John 6:56, *menō* describes the community of life between Father and Son and also the disciples' sharing in Christ's life and works. The words "abide in me, and I in him" indicate a union which is communion, a sharing of Christ's life and works. In placing emphasis on the words *koinonia* (fellowship) and *menō* (abide in), Hooker avoided the suggestion of a union that would destroy identity of one or both of the participants. He was also avoiding reference to fellowship based upon mere kinship. This fellowship which we have with Christ is such that identity as individuals is enhanced and not destroyed. But it is more than mere kinship. It involves a real *participation* and *communion* with God in Christ.

Communion concerns, first and foremost, participation in the divine life. Indeed, Scripture and the tradition of the early church identify God not only as the source of all life, but as life itself. In the Johannine writings, Christ is the bestower of life and he is life in person. For Gregory of Nyssa, God is not only the origin and source of life: God *is* life. Therefore to live is to participate in life and also to participate in God. By the same reasoning Gregory of Nyssa holds that since God is all good, to practice virtue is to participate in God. In his *Life of Moses*, he puts it simply: "Whoever pursues virtue participates in nothing other than God, because he is true virtue." It follows, also, that to be is to participate in God, who is true being.

Hooker's way of putting this is different and important. He speaks of God as having "his influence into the very essence of all things." And he continues:

> Of him all things have both received their first being
> and their continuance to be that which they are. All
> things are therefore partakers of God, they are his
> offspring, his influence is in them, and the personal
> wisdom of God is for that very cause said to excel in
> nimbleness or agility, to pierce into all pure and
> subtle spirits, to go through all, and to reach unto
> every thing which is (*Laws*, V.56.5).

It is of vital importance that this theological statement of Hooker's be taken seriously. As we remarked earlier, creation is only apparently fragmented; in reality it is whole. Creation, and all of life, comes from God. God penetrates and influences all that is by virtue of creation. And yet, as Hooker is quick to point out, creation is flawed and life is maimed. Our resistance to God's influence is a major cause of the imperfection; our imperfection in turn contributes toward our resistance. We so distort life that our life is less than it is meant to be, less than that fullness of life as it is in God and as it comes from God.

Christian spirituality involves the awakening of the human mind and spirit to their essential dependence upon God, and God's reign over all of life. Christian spirituality concerns our dawning and growing awareness of the essential worth, the divinity of all that is, as well as the purpose that God has for all of life. Christ came from God to restore fallen life to true life, to restore fallen being to true being, marred goodness to true goodness. That is, Christ came to empower fuller participation in the divine life.

In a very real sense our restoration, which is to be understood in terms of *metanoia*, or turning from self-preoccupation to the worship of God, is participation that at its fullest issues in adoration. Evelyn Underhill regarded adoration as the first step in self-transcendence. Adoration is "the response 'of awe-struck love' to the overshadowing Reality of God, the 'first response of the awakened creature.'" What Underhill says reminds me of Charlotte Salomon and of the painting she left behind that showed her standing at a window looking out, not at the death camp to which she was destined, but at trees and the sky, the doomed young girl crying out "God, my God, how beautiful it is." At that moment Salomon transcended her preoccupation with self, open to participation and ready for communion with God and with others in and through the love of God.

Anglican spirituality at its best is careful to maintain the necessary interrelationship between corporate worship and private devotion. It recognizes that the fullest communion with God is only realized as the Christian participates regularly in the liturgical life of the church — in a *particular* church, in the midst of God's people — while at the same time reading the Scriptures and praying from the heart in a disciplined routine of personal prayer. One action supports the other. As Harvey Guthrie says, the personal devotions of the Christian are meant to enhance and support corporate worship, for as we have noted along the way the tendency of spirituality is toward the corporate, toward participation, toward that wholeness which is reality. As spirituality is essentially social, so Anglican spirituality presumes an attitude of openness — first toward God, and then through God to one another. Such openness is a welcoming spirit, allowing the Holy Spirit to work in our midst, drawing us close to God and closer to one another in God.

In the *Book of Common Prayer* mutual participation is fostered by the sacraments. Frederick Denison Maurice characterized baptism as the sacrament of "constant union." It both witnesses to that communion which each person has with God, by virtue of being alive, and to the joining of the individual to the people of God, in whom and through whom the Holy Spirit lives and works. The corporate nature of this sacrament of initiation is unmistakable. In Anglican tradition, baptism is the sacrament of justification in which our sanctification begins. It stands for that justification and acceptance which we have from God and which restores us to communion with our creator as he is revealed in Jesus Christ. Baptism is the gift of the Holy Spirit; Hooker dares to speak of the "infusion" of the Holy Spirit. Thus the Spirit is in us and with us from the beginning of our life in Christ, as we are both justified and accepted.

The Holy Communion is the sacrament that maintains us in the fellowship with God that baptism initiates. The eucharist was viewed by Richard Hooker as the sacrament of mutual participation, "that we may evermore dwell in him, and he in us" (not *I* in Christ and Christ in *me*). To be maintained in constant fellowship with God, no matter how unevenly, is to be in communion with the members of Christ's body, the church. Growth in the Spirit, which is the fruit of faithful eucharistic practice, is a mutual growth that we experience with others around the common table. The Catechism in the 1979 *Book of Common Prayer* describes the Lord's Supper and its benefits in terms of the forgiveness of sins; it speaks of "strengthening our union with Christ and with one another and the foretaste of the heavenly banquet which is our nourishment in eternal life." This concise and yet rich statement is expressive of the understanding of Cranmer and Andrewes, as well as of the New Testament and the early church.

Our saving relationship with God and with one another, in the liturgy and in life as a whole, is fostered by both contrition and thanksgiving. The two actions become a rhythm that permeates the Prayer Book from 1549 on, and serves to cultivate our spirituality when it informs our daily lives, issuing in words and deeds of sacrificial love and service. In the service of Holy Communion this rhythm is the work of the Spirit in and through word and sacrament, bringing the faithful to contrition, repentance, and amendment of life. This discipline of contrition and praise strengthens the faithful to eat the "lively food," to participate in Christ and he in them. Thus fed with the bread of life, the faithful give thanks through godly lives of mutual, loving, "charitable" communion in all of their relationships with others. The

Holy Communion is instrumental in the formation and preservation of community, the *societas Christiana*, which is the aim and the end of human existence on earth.

With these considerations in mind, it is possible to say that the *Book of Common Prayer* is *the* instrument in Anglicanism for spiritual growth. It is the *regulum*, a rule of life in the genre of the great monastic rules. To live by this rule is to acknowledge the righteous God and to experience the unseen breaking in upon the seen in order to transform it. Those who worship with this book are to be conformed to Christ (*metanoia*), and this saving action is experienced within the community of the faithful. Through the liturgical drama, in which the Holy Spirit is at work, the faithful are engaged in communion with one another through the intimacy of the particular congregation (the *microcosm*) and in the growing reality of global community (the *macrocosm*). The communion with Christ established through the liturgical action issues in thanksgiving and in words and deeds of sacrificial love and service by which the faithful members of Christ's body become part of Christ's continuing mission and ministry.

The Roots of Anglican Spirituality

To look back to the formative period of Anglicanism is to appreciate the positive influences of its tradition upon present practice. It is also to be liberated from bondage to the past, for in facing tradition squarely we are able to say no as well as yes to the elements of the past that continue, in effect, into the present. We therefore look back to the sixteenth and seventeenth centuries, to theologians, preachers, and poets. Above all we look to the *Book of Common Prayer* together with the English Bible, which is so intimately and regularly involved in the use of the Prayer Book. Since our concern is for spirituality it is important that we focus attention upon the effects of the liturgy upon the people of the Elizabethan and Jacobean Church: that focus should reveal the spirit of their faith and life and enhance spirituality, which we have identified as having to do with communion with

God and with one another through the activity of the Holy Spirit. Since evidence concerning the spirituality of the ordinary people of the sixteenth and seventeenth centuries is scarce, we shall have to concentrate upon those people who have left some record concerning their spiritual journeys.

The metaphysical poets of the first half of the seventeenth century provide the best evidence. Furthermore, they are very much in tune with spirituality as we have been considering it. They emphasize communion and wholeness. For them mind and feeling were unified. Those whom we shall consider lived with and were influenced by the *Book of Common Prayer* while being familiar with other traditions. They became, after difficult spiritual journeys, priests of the Church of England: John Donne (1572-1631), the dean of St. Paul's Cathedral, London, and George Herbert (1593-1633), priest of the parishes of Fugglestone St. Peter and Bemerton St. Andrew, near Salisbury. They both conducted worship day by day using the 1559 Prayer Book as it was amended at the beginning of the reign of King James I. Both wrote poetry which expresses the main elements of Anglican spirituality, and which has influenced others in the development of spirituality from the seventeenth century to this day.

Revelation and Response: Scripture and Prayer

It is important to begin here with the objective action of God, for without God's revelation of himself and his enabling grace, there could be no response, no communion, and thus no spirituality in the sense in which we have been considering it. God's action in reaching out toward humanity initiates communion with God in Christ, through the activity of the Holy Spirit, and with persons who enjoy mutual relationship through their communion with God.

Richard Hooker, in explaining the *Book of Common Prayer* in Book V of his magnum opus, *Of the Laws of Ecclesiastical Polity* (1597), wrote of the dynamic action of God reaching toward humanity and arousing a response. The imagery he uses is medieval and Ptolemaic. We might wish to express ourselves differently; if we did, we should have to find some image that preserved the dynamic action contained here. Hooker has in mind Scripture and prayer, God and the faithful.

> Between the throne of God in heaven and his Church upon earth here militant if it be so that Angels have their continual intercourse, where should we find the same more verified than in these two ghostly exercises, the one '*Doctrine*', the other '*Prayer*'? For what is the assembling of the Church to learn, but the receiving of Angels descended from above? What to pray, but the sending of Angels upward? His heavenly inspirations and our holy desires are as so many Angels of intercourse and commerce between God and us (V.23.1).

The dynamic involved in angels descending with doctrine and angels ascending with prayer is clearly at the heart of the Prayer Book daily offices. The lessons and psalms of Scripture equal doctrine; canticles and prayers equal prayer.

Much could be noted in George Herbert's collection of poems, *The Temple* (1633) concerning the descent of doctrine through the reading of Scripture and the proc-

lamation of God's Word in preaching. A poem in his collection entitled *Sacred Grove* conveys most vividly his
understanding. It is called "In S. Scripturas":

> O what spirit, what fiery whirlwind
> Takes my bones and stirs
> My deepest thoughts? When I was resting
> Near my door not long ago,
> And it was evening, did I
> Swallow a falling star? And is it
> Trying to escape, not knowing how
> In this disgraceful lodging to be hidden?
> Have I in sipping honey
> Consumed the bee, in eating up
> The house eaten up the mistress of the house?
> Not bee, not star has penetrated me.
> Most Holy Writ, it's you who've traveled through
> All the dark nooks and hidden pleats
> Of the heart, the alleys and the curves
> Of flying passion. Ah, how wise and skilled you are
> To slip through these paths, windings, knots.
> The spirit that has reared the building
> Knows it best.[16]

For Herbert, as for other sensitive Christians of the time,
the Holy Scriptures were not simply a book to study in
order to learn what is right and good and true. In the
Book of Homilies the sermon called "A Fruitful Exhortation to the Reading and Knowledge of Holy Scripture"
begins with an exhortation to study the Scripture in order
that we may draw "out of that fountain and well of truth"
all necessary doctrine. But then the sermon goes on to
say that Scripture should be constantly in our hands, eyes,
ears, mouths, and hearts. "For the Scripture of God

is the heavenly meat of our souls. . . . The words of
holy Scripture be called the words of everlasting life. . . .
They are lively, quick, and mighty in operation, and
sharper than any two-edged sword, and entereth through
even unto the dividing asunder of the soul and the spirit,
of the joints and the marrow [Heb. iv.12]." It was commonly believed that the Holy Spirit was the author of
Scripture, and consequently that correct interpretation of
Scripture depended upon the operation of the Holy Spirit
within us, in accord with our spirits. Scripture then
could be interpreted as Herbert understood it. It was
lively. It could penetrate the reader or hearer, take their
bones and stir their deepest thoughts, traveling through
the paths, windings, knots of flying passion. Nothing
could escape the scrutiny or the power of God's holy
Word. It could bring judgment and condemnation, conversion and salvation.

From our perspective in the twentieth century, we
might be inclined to identify justly what Herbert describes here as "spirit" and "fiery whirlwind" with the
gospel good news as it is expressed in Scripture. Indeed,
to a degree Scripture and liturgy are inseparable, the Holy
Spirit at work in and through both. Cranmer believed
that liturgy had to be fundamentally Scripture, or scrip-
tural. Under the influence of the Holy Spirit, liturgy is
the vehicle by which Scripture is transmitted through
drama most effectively to influence the lives of people
and to bring about transformation. We should imagine
Scripture as an objective, forceful, penetrating spirit,
which sets in motion that mutual participation so vital to
Christian spirituality. Such a spirit calls for a response,
and that response is prayer.

When we turn to prayer, we first of all confront in
George Herbert's prose work, *A Priest to the Temple*, a

description of the parson at prayer. Here the parson is instructed to lead the people in prayer, "presenting with himself the whole Congregation, whose sins he then bears, and brings with his own to the heavenly altar to be bathed and washed in the sacred laver of Christ's blood." Further on Herbert speaks of the superiority of prayer, the offering up of a reasonable sacrifice, in applying "our powers to the service of him that gives them." Thought and feeling coincide in heart-felt, reasonable prayer, the prayer expressing a unified sensibility, powerful in its creation and maintenance.

At the end of *A Priest in the Temple* there is, for use after a sermon, a prayer that is a perfect example of what is meant when we speak of the character and quality of prayer in Anglican tradition. It is a heart-felt response to God's gift of grace as we know it in and through God's Word in Scripture and in liturgy. The Holy Spirit is active in these carefully crafted and yet deeply affective words, as the same Spirit was active in and through the Word.

Blessed be God! and the Father of all mercy! who continueth to pour his benefits upon us. Thou hast elected us, thou hast called us, thou hast justified us, sanctified, and glorified us: Thou wast born for us, and thou livest and diedst for us: Thou hast given us the blessings of this life, and of a better. O Lord! thy blessings hang in clusters, they come trooping upon us! They break forth like mighty waters on every side. And now Lord, thou hast fed us with the bread of life: so man did eat Angels food: O Lord, blesse it: O lord, make it health and strength unto us; still striving and prospering so long within us, until our obedience reach the measure of thy love, who hast done for us as much as may be . . .

The prayer acknowledges that the Word of God, the bread of life, feeds the faithful, bringing health and strength, and is still striving and prospering within them, and will continue to do so "until our obedience reach the measure of thy love," which is to say, "until we all attain . . . to mature manhood, to the measure of the stature of the fulness of Christ" (Ephs. 4:13). Thus did Herbert witness to the fellowship, the communion, the dynamic relationship between God and humanity as begun, maintained, and brought to fruition through the activity of the Holy Spirit.

In *The Temple* there is a poem on the nature of prayer which was written as a sonnet. It begins,

> Prayer the Church's banquet, Angels age,
>> God's breath in man returning to his birth,
>> The soul in paraphrase, heart in pilgrimmage,
> The Christian plummet sounding heav'n
>>> and earth . . .

The nature of prayer is grasped in a series of evocative metaphors. The first quatrain is what we might expect from "Gentle Herbert." Prayer is the church's banquet; through prayer we sit at God's board and are fed, as we are open, available to receive God's saving Word. Prayer is "Angel's age," timeless, lifting us up out of the threescore years and ten, which is our alloted time. Prayer is "God's breath . . . returning." Without God's enabling us through his Word, we cannot pray; as we pray, our prayer returns to God, its source. It is "the soul in paraphrase," the soul opening out, more fully revealing and thus more fully discovering its true self. It is "the Christian plummet." Through prayer we test, sound and come to understand all that is of ultimate worth, seeing both

heaven and earth as through a glass darkly, but nevertheless with a heightened awareness.

The mood is sharply different in the second quatrain.

> Engine against th'Almighty, sinners' tower,
> Reversed thunder, Christ-side-piercing spear,
> The six-days world transposing in an hour,
> A kind of tune, which all things hear and fear . . .

Here we are reminded that prayer controlled by sinful
souls can be used against God, can become the "sinners'
tower," glorifying ourselves rather than glorifying God, a
veritable tower of Babel. "Engine against th' Almighty"
and "Reversed thunder" call to mind Jupiter's thunderbolts, but here it is not a god casting them at mankind.
The thunderbolts of prayer are being cast at God. God
gives the power for this to happen; it is part of his
gracious mercy towards us. This idea contributes to our
understanding of the presence of evil in this world.
Prayer in this sense is the "Christ-side-piercing spear."
The thunderbolt becomes a spear, cast at the Son of God;
Christ is crucified once more. Such is the power of
prayer, by God's grace, such power as could transpose in
an hour that which it took God six days to create. The
quatrain does not close on this bitter note, but rather on a
note of awe. Prayer is "a kind of tune, which all things
hear and fear." The music of the spheres that governs all
things comes to mind, such music as may cause a
metaphysical shudder. Such awe and fear was inspired by
the splitting of the atom and is part of our condition now.
Prayer is like that: in the mouth of the righteous a
glorious power for good; in the mouth of an evil one, a
terrifying, destructive force.

The final sestet turns the corner.

Softness, and peace, and joy, and love, and bliss,
   Exalted Manna, gladness of the best,
   Heaven in ordinary, man well drest,
The Milky Way, the bird of Paradise,
   Church-bells beyond the stars heard,
        the soul's blood,
The land of spices; something understood.

The metaphors are now the reverse of those that went before; we need not stop with each one of them. Prayer is "The Milky Way," the way *to* God. Jupiter, who designed the Milky Way, is called to mind once more. He designed it as a pathway to the palace where he summoned the gods to decide the fate of the world. Herbert's Milky Way of prayer is far superior: it allows the faithful to answer God's summons and so to ascend to God's throne. There one can survey heaven and earth and gain perspective on the present through the revelation of the ultimate meaning of the universe in Scripture and liturgy. Prayer is the bird of paradise, the peacock, the phoenix, enabling human beings to fly, transcending ordinary time and space. Prayer is "Church-bells beyond the stars heard, the soul's blood,/ The land of spices" - and then the metaphors cease. The images seem to pile up upon the last two words of the poem: "something understood."

At the end Herbert has expressed the deeper meaning of prayer. Prayer surpasses all knowledge, all earthly rationality, and bears us into the bliss of communion with God, whose breath prayer is and whose love is expressed in the gift of prayer. For in giving the power to pray, God gives the power to use prayer against the giver, a weapon which in the end disarms its bearer. The final point is that prayer is God's doing; this being so, he hears and understands in ways we cannot altogether comprehend but can only regard with joyful awe. Furthermore, what Herbert does in this poem should warn us against defining prayer in the ways it has been customarily defined all too narrowly. The Prayer Book catechism lists "adoration, praise, thanksgiving, penitence, oblation, intercession, and petition." Yet prayer is so much more than that: it is "something understood." It is that life which we have in Christ, and which we can justly describe as "the life of prayer." It is God's breath returning to its source. Prayer is our communion with God in Christ, more than words and more than mute actions. It is mutal participation, Christ in us and we in Christ.

Journey Towards God: The Life of Prayer

The descent of doctrine and the ascent of prayer is not automatic. Scripture may descend to us, but there is no assurance that we shall respond as God wishes, with an ascent of love in return for divine love. Our response, as Herbert indicates in his sonnet on prayer, may be expressed in terms of anger, "Christ-side-piercing spear." Or we may *wish* to respond with prayer that befits our communion with the Creator, full of awe and praise, and not be able to do it. We may not be available to God's Spirit in such a way that we can turn from self-preoccupation to adoration of our Lord and Savior. John Donne experienced the frustrations of one who knows God's love and cannot respond to that love as he wishes, as he knows he should. The Holy Sonnets are expressive of his struggle. "Batter my heart" is most dramatic, the poet pleading

[54]

with God to effect that which the poet cannot effect of himself:

> Batter my heart, three person'd God; for, you
> As yet but knock, breathe, shine, and seek to mend;
> That I may rise, and stand, o'erthrow me, and bend
> Your force, to break, blow, burn and make me new.
> I, like an usurpt town, to another due,
> Labor to admit you, but Oh, to no end,
> Reason your viceroy in me, me should defend,
> But is captiv'd, and proves weak or untrue,
> Yet dearly I love you, and would be lov'd fain,
> But am betroth'd unto your enemy,
> Divorce me, untie, or break that knot again,
> Take me to you, imprison me, for I
> Except you enthrall me, never shall be free,
> Nor ever chaste, except you ravish me.

In the language of the times, Donne is in bondage to sin, the self's love of self to the exclusion of others, and seems unable to break free and thus to love God and know God's love. Reason was "right reason," by whose light the individual is able to see and do the good. Reason is God's viceroy, but "is captiv'd, and proves weak or untrue." What Donne is pleading for is the dramatic invasion of the Holy Spirit that will liberate him from his bondage - given the sexual language of the poem, it may be from bondage to the lustful, selfish desires of the flesh. What he seems not to know is that the invasion has occurred, the power is there, and what is needed is repentance, forgiveness, and renewal, in order to enter into life-giving communion with God again.

George Herbert knew the same struggle. He stood before the cross of Christ every time he stood before the altar of his parish church. There he would acknowledge God in Christ as the wholly Other, the righteous deity, who gives his life as an atonement for our sins. And yet the would-be disciple resisted the communion, whether through fear of losing control of his life or through a sense of unworthiness. He was, as he believed, in a state of sin, separated from God in Christ and from Christ's beloved in this life.

In "The Thanksgiving," Herbert is so overwhelmed by what God has done for him in the sacrifice of his Son that Herbert feels compelled to make some suitable response. He wants to do something worthy of the forgiveness, the love, the mercy shown by God in Christ on the Cross. His attention is fixed upon the grief that Christ suffered for his sake; he would grieve himself, weep blood, be scourged, but it is no use. He cannot hope to equal the grief his savior knew. His mind wanders as he thinks what he might do in return for what Christ, perhaps, will do for him.

> If thou does give me honor, men shall see,
>   The honor does belong to thee.
> I will not marry; or, if she be mine,
>   She and her children shall be thine . . . .
> My bosom friend, if he blaspheme thy Name,
>   I will tear thence his love and fame.
> One half of me being gone, the rest I give
>   Unto some Chapel, die or live.

But then his mind inevitably returns to that which he cannot ignore for long.

> As for thy passion - But of that anon,
>   When with the other I have done.

[56]

And once more he figures what he can do for what God in Christ is doing or will do.

> For thy predestination I'll contrive
> That three years hence, if I survive,
> I'll build a spittle, or mend common ways,
> But mend mine own without delays.

Herbert continues until, at the end, he is drawn back to the cross.

> Nay, I will read thy book, and never move
> Till I have found therein thy love,
> Thy art of love, which I'll turn back on thee:
> O my dear Saviour, Victory!
> Then for thy passion - I will do for that -
> Alas, my God, I know not what.

He has gazed upon the suffering Christ on the cross and he has felt his heart breaking, as we know from the poem "The Altar." He has felt his heart breaking as he felt divine grace descending upon him, and has wept tears of contrition and somber joy. But Herbert is a proud man, born to a family of distinction, a fellow and orator at his university. He has aspired to the grandeur of the royal court and has served in his country's parliament. He will strive to do that which is worthy of God's great gift of love. But in the process he resists the full impact of divine love, such love as has power to change him, to liberate him from sin, from self-preoccupation. He is determined to earn God's love and enter into communion with head held high, in control of his life and of his destiny. But when his mind returns again to the suffering Christ, he is bereft.

Another poem, "The Reprisal," continues the struggle but with a deeper, further understanding.

> I have considered it, and find
> There is no dealing with thy mighty passion:
> For though I die for thee, I am behind;
>   My sins deserve the condemnation.
>
> O make me innocent, that I
> May give a disentangled state and free:
> And yet thy wounds still my attempts defy,
>   For by thy death I die for thee.
>
> Ah! was it not enough that thou
> By thy eternal glory did out go me?
> Could thou not grief's sad conquests me allow,
>   But in all victories overthrow me?
>
> Yet by confession will I come
> Into thy conquest: though I can do nought
> Against thee, in thee I will overcome
>   The man, who once against thee fought.

Herbert is brought to the realization that there is nothing he can do to warrant God's mercy. There is no dealing with Christ's passion. All that Herbert can do is to recognize the state of his sin, and his finitude, and by confession enter into his Lord's conquest of sin and death. Thus may he partake of divine life and inherit eternal life.

It is important to realize here that the poet's yielding control over his own life and destiny, involving his availability toward love, does not involve the destruction of the self or the transmutation of George Herbert into someone or something else. In the process of yielding, of experiencing that contrition that leads to repentance, confession, and newness of life, he is growing in grace and in that true being that is his in Christ Jesus. He is becoming more fully the George Herbert that from the beginning God intended him to be. His participation in Christ's passion through the suffering we call contrition, and Christ's victory through the forgiveness that issues in new life, enables his communion with God and with others in God. The arrogance of self has been confronted and overcome.

Here we have a key to understanding a poem that precedes "The Thanksgiving" and "The Reprisal." "The Altar" is a pattern poem, in the shape of an altar-table, to be read in the spirit of one who enters the church building and sees the altar illuminated by a beam of sunshine. The altar is the table on which the Holy Communion is offered and administered and it is simultaneously the cross of sacrifice and the poet's heart, the altar of the heart.

A broken ALTAR, Lord, thy servant rears,
Made of a heart, and cemented with tears:
  Whose parts are as thy hand did frame;
  No workman's tool hath touch'd the same.
    A heart alone
    Is such a stone,
    As nothing but
    Thy pow'r doth cut.
    Wherefore each part
    Of my hard heart
    Meets in this frame
    To praise thy Name:
  That, if I chance to hold my peace,
  These stones to praise thee may not cease.
O let thy blessed S A C R I F I C E be mine,
And sanctify this A L T A R to be thine.

In experiencing Christ's passion, the poet is already in the process of entering into communion with God and others. His heart is broken and thus accessible, available for the working of the Holy Spirit, and his contrition issues in praise. This is the necessary rhythm of contrition and praise that we find in the *Book of Common Prayer*, and it does not occur once for all time.

We live in a fragmented, broken world, a world in bondage to sin, death, and meaninglessness. We are not apart from this world, but in the world as persons whose citizenship is in heaven. Living in this world, *simul justus et peccator*, as Luther said, righteous and sinful, we by grace live by this necessary rhythm of contrition and praise, contrition and praise, to eternal life.

In one of his most effective poems, Herbert's problem is revealed not as prideful self-assertion, but rather as a stubborn sense of unworthiness, a wallowing in contrition without being able to experience forgiveness and to sing out in praise of God. Hooker spoke of this condition as that of over-scrupulosity and regarded it as great a sin as pride. In the poem Herbert has in mind the Last Judgment and the messianic banquet, the final communion in Heaven when, as we read in Luke 12:37, God "shall gird himself, and make them to sit down to meat, and will come forth and serve them." Herbert incorporated this in his poem "Love (III)."

> Love bade me welcome: yet my soul drew back,
>   Guilty of dust and sin.
> But quick-ey'd Love, observing me grow slack
>   From my first entrance in,
> Drew nearer to me, sweetly questioning,
>   If I lack'd any thing.
> A guest, I answer'd, worthy to be here:
>   Love said, You shall be he.
> I the unkind, ungrateful? Ah my dear,
>   I cannot look on thee.
> Love took my hand, and smiling did reply,
>   Who made the eyes but I?
> Truth Lord, but I have marr'd them: let my shame
>   Go where it doth deserve.
> And know you not, says Love, who bore the blame?
>   My dear, then I will serve.
> You must sit down, says Love, and taste my meat:
>   So I did sit and eat.

To the very last, the welcomed guest seeks to retain control over his life and destiny. When Love, the host, explains that his guest's shame has been canceled through Love's sacrificial self-offering, and the guest knows he has no choice but to stay, the guest announces that he will serve. But Love counters, saying, "You must sit down." It is the Lord who shall serve the guest. The final resignation occurs, which is also the final resolution: "So I did sit and eat."

Spirituality involves humility, openness, and availability. Both Herbert and Donne struggled with pride, the pride that cannot accept God's loving forgiveness once contrition and repentance are operative in the individual's life. They were in need of help, and help was there for them in the prayer book worship of the community. In Morning Prayer and in the Holy Communion the gathered people of God were reminded of their need to repent, said the General Confession, and heard forgiveness pronounced. In the Holy Communion the words were these: "Have mercy upon you, pardon and deliver you from all your sins, confirm and strengthen you in all goodness, and bring you to everlasting life . . . " What is anticipated in confession is thanksgiving; indeed, thanksgiving is the goal.

Thanksgiving, not repentance, is meant to be the dominant note in the Christian life. Elizabethan Christians were reminded of this in the third exhortation of the 1559 Prayer Book:

And above all you must give most humble and hearty thanks to God the Father, the Son, and the Holy Ghost, for the redemption of the world by the death and passion of our Savior Christ both God and man; who did humble himself, even to the death upon the cross for us miserable sinners, which lay in darkness and shadow of death, that he might make us the children of God, and exalt us to everlasting life.

Spirituality and the Sacraments

The reverence for Scripture and sacraments at the heart of Anglican spirituality cultivates that communion which is essential to human existence, and which for Christians is necessary for the salvation of the people of God. The fathers of Anglican tradition during the sixteenth and seventeenth centuries understood this, not in twentieth-century terms, but in their own equally valid terms. Thomas Cranmer emphasized communion with God and with one another in the local congregation. John Jewel, the Bishop of Salisbury who died in 1570, wrote of the sacraments as the visible words of God. Richard Hooker made much of the doctrine of participation. Lancelot Andrewes, the Bishop of Winchester, emphasized the doctrine of sacrifice. All regarded the sacraments as "medicines of grace," graciously provided to assist fallen human beings in that process of *metanoia* where they are turned from their present bondage to enjoy new life in Christ. Attention was naturally focused on Christ — upon the cross revealing to all mankind the mercy and love of God, which is powerful to arouse contrition and to empower the faithful to live as God meant them to live. These Anglican divines make much of the cross in sermons and writings, in prayers and other devotions. For them the cross was the supreme symbol of divine love, of the amazing communion between the God of the universe and fallen humanity.

The Holy Communion was the sacrament of sanctification. By it, the souls and bodies of the faithful were fed as they encountered the Word made flesh, and in the encounter died to sin and rose to righteousness. To be partakers of the body and blood of Christ was to enter into his sacrifice, thereby to die to sin and to rise with him to newness of life. In baptism and in the Holy Communion the *passion* of Christ was emphasized by word and by liturgical action. The prayers of thanksgiving for each of the sacraments in the sixteenth-century Prayer Book relate the saving drama to the renewal of lives in Christ. After baptism the faithful give thanks "that he [who is baptised] is made partaker of the death of thy son, so he may be partaker of his resurrection," and after the Eucharist the faithful give thanks that by partaking of "the spiritual food of the most precious blood" of Christ, we are assured of God's love towards us, our incorporation into the mystical body of the Church, and are made heirs "through hope, of thy everlasting kingdom, by the merits of thy most precious death and passion."

Jewel, Hooker, and Andrewes, when they passed beyond the controversial issues of their day to what was for them of greatest importance in the sacraments, focused on the passion of Christ. Their prose became poetic, exhibiting that unified sensibility of thought and feeling which was to be found in Anglican spirituality in its formative period. Thus Jewel, in a sermon preached in his cathedral at Salisbury, exhorted: "Let us remember, Christ was forsaken, scorned, buffeted, crucified, and left upon the cross. . . ." By the power of this remembrance through his Word, Christ speaks "to thee, and calls, saying: Behold, O man, thus have I sought thee: these things I suffer for thy sake, that thou shouldest eat my flesh and drink my blood, and be made one with me. . . ." Therefore, Jewel continued, "Let us die with Christ, let us be crucified unto the world. Let us be holy eagles, and soar above. . . ." Let us offer up our bodies a living, pure, holy, and acceptable sacrifice to God. So shall we be partakers of Christ, and of his resurrection."[17] Thinking of Holy Communion, Richard Hooker wrote that "the very letter of the word of Christ gives plain security that these mysteries do as nails fasten us to his very cross, that by them we draw out, as touching efficacy, force and virtue, even the blood of his goared side. . . ." (*Laws*, V.67.12). Lancelot Andrewes set forth a vision of Christ on the cross, water and blood flowing from his wounded side. He said, "Mark it out and suffer it not to run to waste, but receive it." Out of Christ's pierced side, "God 'opened a fountain of water, to the House of Israel for sin and for uncleanness;' of the fulness whereof we all have received in the Sacrament of our Baptism." The blood flowing from Christ's side, which is "the blood of the New Testament," "we may receive this day; for it will run in the high and holy mysteries of the Body and Blood of Christ. There may we be partakers of the flesh of the Morning Hart, as upon this day killed. There may we be partakers of 'the cup of salvation,' 'the precious blood' 'which was shed for the remission of our sins.'"[18]

The spirituality reflected in these quotations from Jewel, Hooker, and Andrewes is centered on the cross of Christ and on the sacraments as instruments of salvation conveying the grace of the divine passion, the holy, healing sacrifice, rooted in Scripture and in the *Book of Common Prayer*. George Herbert's understanding of spirituality and the sacraments is very much along these lines. When writing on Holy Baptism, Herbert turned to the cross as he understood it in the light of Easter and the Resurrection. In "H. Baptism (I)" we have an example of his thinking:

> As he that sees a dark and shady grove,
>   Stays not, but looks beyond it on the sky;
> So when I view my sins, mine eyes remove

[65]

> More backward still, and to that water fly,
> Which is above the heav'ns, whose spring and vent
>   Is in my dear Redeemer's pierced side.
>   O blessed streams! either ye do prevent
> And stop our sins from growing thick and wide,
> Or else give tears to drown them, as they grow.
>   In you Redemption measures all my time,
>   And spreads the plaster equal to the crime.

The poet, beset by a constant awareness of his sins, remembers his baptism and the cleansing water which flowed from the pierced side of the crucified Christ, water which either stops our sins or drowns them (*baptismos*) "as they grow." Redemption in and through Christ, to whom the Christian is joined, covers all of life and provides healing "equal to the crime." That is to say, the new life in Christ which is begun in baptism continues through all of life. For in baptism we are incorporated into Christ and his victory; however much we sin afterward, that one baptism is sufficient. It covers all.

In "H. Baptism (II)" Herbert describes the necessary condition for the continuance of the fruits of baptism and of justification by means of sanctification. The poet is concerned both with infant baptism and the Christian life, and most emphatically with the latter. He is remembering his baptism as an infant and the implications of it for his whole life, especially the fact that infant baptism indicates the objective action of God, laying hold of the infant and antedating "faith in me" - faith before it was actual, in the sense of cognitive formulation and assent. In the second stanza of the poem he prays to remain as a little child, "soft and supple to thy will,/ Small to my self, to others mild,/ Behither [short of] ill." In the final stanza he prays that as his flesh ages his soul may remain childlike. "The growth of flesh is but a blister;/ Childhood is health."

The fruition of the Christian life is not to be found in sophistication, refinement and learning such as the world knows and values. Herbert takes seriously the gospel reading for "The Ministration of Baptism" in the prayer book of his day, and especially the words of Jesus, "Whosoever doth not receive the kingdom of God as a little child, he shall not enter therein" (Mk. 10). Growing into the fullness of Christ is growing into that simple trust, that childlike trust that Christ had in his Father - not without qualms, but steadfast to the end. And thus baptism stands for God's acceptance of us before we have any developed faith, while we have a simple child's faith, and before we have any merits of our own, depending wholly on Christ's merits. Baptism also stands for the reality of new life in Christ, the child-like trust, the "supple will," the growth of humility ("Small to my self") and of kindness and gentleness to others ("to others mild").

There are three poems at the end of *The Temple* concerning the Holy Communion, chiefly exhorting the Christian to come to the feast and at God's board partake of the saving food and drink. They reflect the influence of the Prayer Book exhortation, in particular that which has as its focus the Parable of the Great Feast (Lk. 14:16-24). They are "The Invitation," "The Banquet," and a poem that we have already considered, "Love (III)." The first two command our attention now and can be considered together.

The poet's point, made simply and eloquently, is that although we are taught to understand how dangerous it is to take the body and blood of Christ unworthily, yet we must still believe that God is merciful to forgive and that the sacraments have been provided not for our condemnation, but that we might grow in grace. Therefore, as Herbert says in "The Invitation,"

> Come ye hither All, whom pain
> Doth arraign
> Bringing all your sins to sight:
> Taste and fear not: God is here
> In this cheer,
> And on sin doth cast the fright.

The poet speaks as though he has gone out and has invited all of those whom he has encountered, calling them to the feast, including gluttons, drunkards, those "whom pain doth arraign," those "whom joy doth destroy," and those "whose love is your dove."

> Lord I have invited all
> And I shall
> Still invite, still call to thee
> For it seems but just and right
> In my sight
> Where is All, there All should be.

The second poem, "The Banquet," is a delicate, lyrical poem that is logically related to "The Invitation." Through the banquet feast, the poet welcomes the "Bread of Life." This is food which fills the soul and transforms it, overcoming sin not by bitter judgment but rather by sweetness - the fragrance divine subduing the stench of sin. It is evident that this sweet odor is not ordinary.

> Only God, who gives perfumes,
> Flesh assumes,

And with it perfumes my heart.

The perfume that saves — the scent divine, by which Herbert means Christ — is powerful because "as Pomanders and wood/ Still are good,/ Yet being bruis'd are better scented," so the Christ is more powerful to save because he has been bruised and broken.

> God, to show how far his love
>   Could improve,
> Here, as broken, is presented.

The "here" refers to the feast, the Holy Communion, the table of sacrifice, where bread is broken, the body bruised and broken, for our sakes, broken to be distributed that those who partake of it may be united to their Lord and enjoy that Holy Communion that is life itself.

The poet then reflects: When I had forgotten my heavenly birth by baptism into Christ, and wallowed in my self-indulgent ways, drowning in the delights of earth, God made flesh and incarnate came to me and found me where I was, "on the ground." God raises me up, giving me wine, his blood spilled for me, to drink. Now, although I am unworthy, being "low and short,/ Far from court...," I begin to fly, "wine becomes a wing at last," and I am transported to heaven and into communion with the Lord my God. What we have here answers the plea of the poem called "Praise (I)":

> I go to Church; help me to wings, and I
>   Will thither fly;
>   Or, if I mount unto the sky,
>   I will do more.

In "The Banquet" the poet says that with this wine, the blood of Christ received in the sacrament,

> alone I fly
> To the sky:
> Where I wipe mine eyes, and see
> What I seek, for what I sue;
> Him I view
> Who hath done so much for me.

In the final stanza, Herbert stands back in wonder, with praise and thanksgiving, that God is so merciful, stooping down to feed him, giving him drink that he may rise, rise up to God's presence where Christ sits at God's right hand in glory. Let, then, this wonder be the poet's "dittie,/ And take up my lines and life." Once more Herbert reflects the Anglican understanding of the sacrament, for the end or purpose in view, cited at the beginning of the poem ("O what sweetness from the bowl/ Fills my soul") and in the final stanza, is the transformation of the person by means of bread and wine, effective instruments for renewal in Christ. Attention is focused not on the consecrated elements but on the use of them by worthy receivers who are themselves transformed in the use.

The content of "The Banquet" is informed by the sequence of the sixteenth-century Book of Common Prayer, which leads from the Invitation to Confession, Absolution and Comfortable Words, to the Sursum Corda ("Lift up your hearts") and the Communion itself. At the end of it the faithful offer up "ourselves, our souls and bodies," raising their voices in chorus as one voice to sing: "Glory be to God on high." "The Banquet" and "The Invitation" express something of the heart of Anglican spirituality and help to explain why this spirituality is corporate and sacramental, having so much to do with the Prayer Book and the Prayer Book sacraments of baptism and the Holy Communion.

The focus is on the cross, that amazing display of divine love, which liberates the faithful from bondage to sin and death, freeing them for new life, for participation in Christ, in his body the church, and for sacrificial service in this broken world. The light of the cross is reflected in the faces of the faithful who, being signed by the sign of the cross, stretch out their hands in contrition with joy to receive the bread, his body, and to drink the wine, his blood. To be in Christ and to be truly in communion with others, it is incumbent upon Christians to trust in him, letting his Holy Spirit direct them. Thus are Christians made open and available to do, in thanksgiving and with great joy, God's will for them and for his world.

Spirituality and Meditative Style in Early Anglicanism

There was a style of discursive meditation that contributed to the shape of Anglican spirituality in the sixteenth and seventeenth centuries in England. The immediate influence might have been the *Spiritual Exercises* of St. Ignatius of Loyola; the *Introduction to the Devout Life* (1608) and the *Treatise on the Love of God* (1616) of St. Francis de Sales were equally influential. But there is another possibility. Joseph Hall, Bishop of Exeter, published *The Art of Divine Meditation* in 1606, a work which was widely read and often reprinted in the seventeenth century. Hall's teaching was formed not by exposure to the meditative methods of St. Ignatius or St.

Francis, but rather by a source common to them all. This was the *Scala Meditatoria*, of Wessell Gansfort as found in John Mombaer's *Rosetum*, first published in 1494, which was identified with the *Devotio Moderna*, a movement toward a modern form of spirituality in which its devotees placed heavy emphasis on the importance of the feelings as well as the intellect. Here was a protest against the overly-intellectual spirituality of the scholastics. Feeling as well as thought was to be taken seriously. The intellect's meditation upon God's mighty acts was to be experienced and felt, behavior was to be modified, and the faithful were to will and to do that which was pleasing in God's sight. Christian action counted with these revolutionaries more than intellectual prowess, and yet the intellect was still to be taken seriously.

In *The Art of Divine Meditation*, Joseph Hall discusses meditation in three stages: (1) the "entrance," which consists of prayer, the opening of the heart to God, and the choice of a subject for meditation, (2) the "proceeding," or meditation proper, concerned with the intellect (or understanding) and the affections, and (3) the "conclusion," the expression of confidence, thanksgiving, and recommendation "of ourselves to God: wherein the soul doth cheerfully give up itself, and repose wholly upon her Maker and Redeemer; committing herself to him, and to walk worthy of her high and glorious calling."[19]

With regard to the meditation proper, we are advised by Hall to begin with a mental description of the chosen subject, followed by a "division," which is to be "easy and voluntary," and not complex or rigid, "whereby our thoughts shall have more room made for them, and our proceeding shall be more distinct." The division of a meditation on Christ's passion, for example, might consist of a serial consideration of the last words or some other means by which different aspects or different moments in time might be intellectually explored. All of this is done in order that the affections or feelings might be stirred, which Hall speaks of as the "very soul of meditation." In the first part of the meditation we see, for understanding involves sight; in the second part we taste, feel, and are affected by the sweetness or bitterness of our subject and are brought to exclaim, shout, or cry out. This passionate response is followed by an act of contrition or humility and finishes in confession. Hall notes the necessary rhythm of contrition and praise in these words: "It is to be duly observed, how the mind is, by turns depressed and lifted up, being lifted up without estate of Joy it is cast down with complaint [contrition]; lifted up with Wishes, it is cast down with confession: which order doth best hold it in ure and just temper; and maketh it more feeling of the comfort." After confession comes petition, whereby we request at God's hand that "which we acknowledge ourselves unable, and none but God able to perform."

Meditation thus understood concerns something that is common in Christian experience. The arousal of the affections is the end and purpose of both sermons and meditations. Preaching in the sixteenth and seventeenth centuries was generally composed of a presentation of the biblical text, its explication and exposition, together with appropriate citations and the application of both text and exposition to the lives of the parishioners with the intent of arousing the affections and causing some positive action. The similarity between preaching and meditation was due in part to the influence of rhetorical conventions and style. Thomas Wilson, in a text-book on rhetoric published in 1553, wrote: "Affections . . . are none other thing, but a stirring, or forcing of the mind, either to desire, or else to detest, and loath any thing more vehemently than by nature we are commonly wont to do."[20]

There were theological roots, too. Richard Hooker compared sermons to the keys of the kingdom of heaven, to wings for the soul, and to "spurs to the good affections of men" (*Laws*, V.22.1). The sermons of John Jewel, Richard Hooker, and Lancelot Andrewes provide vivid examples of the meditative style in sermon form. A favorite subject of both sermons and meditations during the sixteenth and seventeenth centuries in England was, as might be expected, the passion of Christ. Lancelot Andrewes, in a powerful sermon on Zechariah 12:10 (*"and they shall look upon Me, Whom they have pierced"*), concluded:

> How shall we know that Christ doth thus respect us? Then truly, when fixing both the eyes of our meditation [understanding] 'upon Him that was pierced,' - as it were with one eye upon the grief, the other upon the love wherewith he was pierced, we find by both, or one of these some motion of grace arise in our hearts [affections]: the consideration of His grief piercing our hearts with sorrow, the consideration of His love piercing our hearts with mutual love again.[21]

This is what the great preachers of the time succeeded in doing. They pictured Christ upon the cross for their hearers and engaged the minds of their congregations in considering the meaning of what was there displayed. Some, as Jewel did on occasion, then had Christ speak to the faithful, exhorting them to consider his grief and to enter into his sorrow in order that they may make their confessions, and being stirred in their souls arise to do Christ's work in the world. Such sermons were group meditations, with the congregation so engaged by the preacher's meditation that it became their own meditation. This dynamic of intellect and feeling, understanding and the affections, thought and sensibility is found as well in the *Book of Common Prayer*. The tone of the book is established by its preface, where emphasis is placed on the orderly and regular reading of the scriptures in order that the clergy "by often reading and meditation of God's Word [should] be stirred to godliness themselves, and be more able to exhort others by wholesome doctrine, and to confute them that were adversaries to the truth." Thus Morning Prayer begins with preparation, prayer and contrition, confession and absolution. It then proceeds to instruction of the mind, in lessons and canticles, providing the worshippers with subject matter for meditation, and ends with the creed, the Our Father, versicles and prayers, the response of the faithful, engaging their affections, now aroused, and directing them toward newness of life.

The service of Holy Communion is more complex. It begins with preparation, the Collect for Purity, and self-examination through the recitation of the Ten Commandments. There follow propers (collect, epistle and gospel), subject matter for meditation. The creed is a summary of the gospel and, with the "I believe," an effective response. Then comes the sermon, in which subject and response are rehearsed, explained, exposited, as we have observed, intellect and affections both being engaged, always issuing in some action congruent with new life in Christ. In the light of this sequence, offerings are made, money and prayers for the "whole state of Christ's Church militant here in earth."

Then the process begins again, with preparation involving exhortation, confession, and absolution. The subject matter for meditation follows, being both the central action of the liturgy and the remembrance of the passion of Christ in which the liturgy is rooted. Actions and words dramatize to the faithful the infinite, healing, life-giving love of God displayed on the cross. The faithful are drawn into the drama as they receive the body and blood of Christ, the heavenly mysteries that preserve their bodies and souls unto everlasting life. Their affections are engaged by the sacrificial love of God in Christ. The faithful respond to this love, offering "our selves, our souls and bodies, to be a reasonable, holy, and living sacrifice unto thee, humbly beseeching thee, that all we which be partakers of the Holy Communion, may be filled with thy grace, and heavenly benediction." It remains, in the early Prayer Book to sing out "Glory be to God on high," and to be dismissed with the blessing.

The meditative style, involving as it did both understanding and the affections, reaching the affections through the understanding to effect newness of life, was thus at the heart of Anglican spirituality and of Anglicanism in general. And it has deeply influenced the formation of Anglicanism in part through the metaphysical poets of the seventeenth century.

John Donne and Meditative Style

Any consideration of John Donne's spirituality should take into account his sermons and occasional works such as *Devotions Upon Emergent Occasions*, but for a consideration of mediatative style in Anglicanism, attention should be focused on his "Holy Sonnets," also called

"Divine Meditations," and in particular the sequence of 1633, as determined by Dame Helen Gardner.[22] Some critics have considered these poems in relation to Richard Hooker's discussion of repentance in book VI of his *Laws*: the first six sonnets being said to concern the stimulation of fear and the last six the stimulation of love. Helen Gardner views the sonnets of 1633 as having to do with the Last Things (judgment, death) but sees the influence of the Ignatian method of meditation clearly represented in them. I have myself suggested that the 1633 sequence can be viewed in relation to the Eucharist and to the outline for meditation in Joseph Hall's *The Art of Divine Meditation*.

A. The stage is set: preparatory prayer.

Sonnet 1

B. The agony: contrition with pleading for sacramental grace.

Sonnets 2-5

C. Transition: defiant faith.

Sonnet 6

D. The Cross of Christ: the means of grace.

Sonnets 7-9

E. Conclusion: participation in Christ.

Sonnets 10-12

Sonnet 1 is the "entrance," according to Hall's scheme. The poet recollects himself in God's presence. He was made by God and when he had decayed, Christ's blood redeemed him. He is God's son,

made with thyself to shine,
Thy servant, whose pains thou hast still repaid,

> Thy sheep, thine Image, and till I betray'd
> Myself, a temple of thy Spirit divine . . .

Why then, he asks, is he in the grip of the devil, of evil, who possesses that which is God's by right? Next comes the prayer for God to "rise and for thine own work fight." He ends:

> O I shall soon despair, when I do see
> That thou lov'st mankind well, yet will
> > not choose me.
> And Satan hates me, yet is loath to lose me.

On one level this poem expresses the poet's despair that he shall ever be able to turn to God, unless God first turn to him and move him, free him from bondage to sin. His despair deepens with the thought that God does move others by his love but will not move him, choose him. On another level this poem expresses the poet's desire for God and his readiness, his availability to be chosen. The poem expresses his remorse and the beginnings of contrition and repentance. Thus it is preparation for meditation.

Sonnets 2-5 concern repentance, which Hall stresses as a major precondition to meditation. It is also a precondition to participation in the Lord's Supper, as the *Book of Common Prayer* indicated. Sonnet 4, "At the round earths imagin'd corners," focuses attention upon the Last Judgment. The dead are summoned to take on their bodies and enter into beautitude with God. Thinking of the meaning of the Last Judgment, the poet suggests that the dead be allowed to sleep a while longer

and me mourn a space,
For, if above all these, my sins abound,
'Tis late to ask abundance of thy grace,
When we are there; here on this lowly ground,
Teach me how to repent; for that's as good
As if thou'hadst seal'd my pardon, with thy blood.

Repentance is the key, but if he is to repent he must learn how, be taught by God. True repentance means that his red soul is dyed white by the blood of Christ, blood shed as a sacrifice, an atonement for his sins.

Sonnet 6 ("Death be not proud") is transitional, a strong assertion of faith in the face of assailing doubt. Sonnets 7 through 9 contain subject matter for meditation proper. The ninth is in the Hallsian manner, a meditation on Christ's passion:

What if this present were the worlds last night?
Marke in my heart, O Soule, where thou dost dwell,
The picture of Christ crucified, and tell
Whether that countenance can thee affright,
Teares in his eyes quench the amazing light,
Blood fills his frowns, which from his pierc'd
                          head fell,
And can that tongue adjudge thee unto hell,
Which pray'd forgiveness for his foes fierce spite?
No, no . . . .

Donne ends with the statement that beauty such as Christ's springs from the kindness and mercy of love, while ugliness springs from the opposite, from cruelty and mercilessness. Thus he concludes: "To wicked spirits are horrid shapes assign'd,/ This beauteous form assures a pitious mind." The concluding note is one of quiet, firm assurance and thanksgiving. The God of love forgives repentant sinners. It is the awareness of divine love that makes repentance possible. Thus does God move us.

Sonnets 10 through 12 concern the end and purpose of all. They are akin to Hall's "conclusion," and provide suitable endings for both meditation and the Holy Communion. Sonnet 10 ("Batter my heart") expresses something of the frustration in knowing that God has in meditation and sacrament sought an entrance into one's life, and yet it seems not to have happened. Therefore there is a need for a more violent approach on God's part. Sonnet 11 is quietly affirming:

> Wilt thou love God, as he thee! then digest
> My Soul, this wholesome meditation,
> How God the Spirit, by Angels waited on
> In heaven, doth make his Temple in they breast. . . .
> 'Twas much, that man was made like God before,
> But, that God should be made like man, much more.

This is a poem of thanksgiving for what God has done to free us from bondage to sin and death. He has made his Temple in your breast and makes his presence known to you there with each Holy Communion where Christ dwells in you and you in Christ. This, then, is the recognition that the divine invasion in "Batter my heart" has in fact occurred, and that what is required is recognition of and surrender to that fact.

It is not necessary to interpret these poems in this fashion, which is to read them devotionally and not critically, in order to perceive the way in which both intellect and affections are engaged in them. The poet works with consummate art and wit to involve the reader in his train of thought, the shapes, meanings, and music of the poems. The reader's sensibilities are modified as the mind is stirred, affected to desire that good which alone is ultimate: God as revealed in Jesus Christ.

In these poems Donne was seeking, so it seems to me, for communion with God and with others in God, and thus for liberation from bondage to all that inhibits such communion. That Donne focused attention upon the passion of Christ is not surprising, for there on the cross was displayed God's love and mercy, in the light of which we dare to face the Last Things, judgment and death. The sight of Christ, the Incarnate Lord of all, filled him with gratitude and dread and was powerful to arouse within him that *metanoia*, that contrition and repentance that leads not to despair but to eucharistic, thankful living.

Donne's poetry is focused, thus, on the figure of Jesus. In a sermon for Trinity Sunday, he pleads,

> Love him then, as he is presented to thee here; love the *Lord*, love *Christ*, love *Jesus* . . . I love my Savior as he is *The Lord*; He that studies my salvation; And as *Christ*, made a person able to work my salvation; but when I see him in the third motion, *Jesus*, accomplishing my salvation, by an actual death, I see those hands stretched out, that stretched out the heavens . . . .

This is not the end of the matter, however it might seem that it would be. For the context in which salvation is realized, according to Donne's understanding, is the church:

> There is no name given under heaven whereby you should be saved, there are no other means whereby

salvation should be applied in his name given, but those which he has instituted in his Church . . . .

The Holy Sonnets must finally be understood in relation to that participation or fellowship which we have in the church, the community of faith. The personal struggle to which those poems give witness is not waged in solitude, but is surrounded and enabled by a great company of people of the church militant here in earth and of the church triumphant in heaven. Donne revered the church. In his "Hymn to Christ, at the Author's last going into Germany," the church is depicted as a "torn ship," sorely divided, but it is, nevertheless, God's ark, Christ's spouse, in which the poet and all others who follow Christ live and grow in grace.

Anglican spirituality is concerned with communion, between God and the faithful and in the local congregation that meets to worship using the *Book of Common Prayer*. In the period of its formation during the sixteenth and seventeenth centuries, the Prayer Book became the *regulum* of the people composing the Church of England. This was as true in the colonies, in Virginia and elsewhere, as it was in the motherland. The Prayer Book dominated spirituality, and with its emphasis on common prayer and Holy Communion, its concern for the common weal and the building of the *societas Christiana*, assured that private devotions alone were not the be-all and end-all of Christian spirituality. It is true that in Herbert and Donne we have seen men who struggled intensely as individuals to secure and perfect communion with God. But in both cases there was a keen awareness of the fact that the struggle took place in the context of the church and that their personal quests could be successfully pursued only when they were upheld by the common worship of the people of God. Herbert, in naming his collection of verse *The Temple*, meant not only the individual Christian as the temple of the Holy Spirit, but also the church. Donne, realizing that personal devotions in and of themselves were deficient, and at times were even impossible, turned to the church at prayer. And Lancelot Andrewes' great compendium of private devotions, the *Preces Privatae*, did not consist of *extempore* prayers but was carefully constructed out of the Scriptures and the public liturgies of Christendom, including the *Book of Common Prayer*. Yet there was great emphasis placed upon a personal, howbeit communal, participation in Christ. It is this communion, involving Christ (the object of devotion), the individual in community (the worshipper), and prayer as the current of devotion, including meditation and the sacraments, as all are viewed in this twentieth century, to which we now turn our attention.

The Christ We Know

Christian spirituality is concerned with communion. That communion primarily has to do with the encounter between two personal beings, God and the human individual in the context of the community of the faithful. For Anglicanism during its formative years of the sixteenth and seventeenth centuries, God was known most immediately and intimately as revealed in Jesus Christ. Furthermore, the sacraments and common piety tended to emphasize Christ upon the cross. The Jesus of the miracles and the triumphant risen Lord were understood in relation to the great sacrifice of God in Jesus Christ on the cross, from whence shone forth the gracious mercy and love of God to sinful people. The cross is the emblem of forgiveness and of atonement. It points the way in which the disciples of Jesus in any age should go: walking

the way of the cross, which is to live the life of sacrificial love and service.

Yet the modern Christian asks, who is this Jesus
Christ? What do we know of him? How do we know anything of him? The doubting modern then turns upon the
other end of the encounter. Who are we humans? Do we
actually exist, or are we figments of some imagination?
What is our true condition? Are we sinful or are we
simply pawns in a game over which we have no control?
Why do we feel that this world is broken beyond repair?
Why are we sometimes so buoyantly optimistic? How
seriously can I take Descartes' *cogito ergo sum*? How can
I be sure? Haven't I manufactured a god to suit myself,
picking and choosing bits and pieces of deity here and
there to create a god who will do what I want to have
done? These questions indicate a crisis of the consciousness-centered personality.

There is also that which flows between God and a
doubting person: doctrine and prayer. In this meeting we
speak of the operation of the Holy Spirit and of worship,
or prayer. But what of the Holy Spirit and what of
prayer? Sometimes we feel as though there is nothing
there; when we think there is something there, we may be
fantasizing. In what follows in this chapter, we shall ex-
plore these areas of doubt. But before we do, it is of
vital importance that we realize the legitimate place of
doubt in Christian spirituality. Stephen Sykes provides a
clue when he says:

> The Judaeo-Christian spirituality . . . strongly en-
> courages the utmost honesty in dealing with God, and
> the tradition of the negative way affords support to
> those who enter the experience of doubt and despair.
> The *sacrificium intellectus* is less a confinement of

the mental horizons to those of comfortable religiosity, than an engagement of the whole self in a quest for truth.[23]

Indeed, there would be no faith without doubt, for if we could prove the things of faith empirically, faith would fade into certainty. Christian spirituality involves faith, and the basis and context for that faith will be the final matter with which we deal in this chapter.

Imagining Who Christ Is

No one painted a picture or sculpted a statue or took a photograph of Jesus while he was on earth. Nor did anyone leave for posterity a biography of Jesus. The gospels are not the sort of thing we now look for and expect in a biography of an important world figure. In the New Testament we have the proclamation of God's mighty acts in and through Jesus of Nazareth for the sake of a world in bondage to sin and death. Whom, then, do we see in our imaginations as we enjoy fellowship with and enter into union with Jesus Christ? It may be suggested that it is not necessary to have a mental image of Jesus, and yet insofar as the communion of which we speak is personal it must be communion involving *persons*, one with another. Since for us in our day-to-day experience people are not bodiless spirits, but minds and spirits integrally related to bodies, it is not out of keeping with Christian spirituality to ask, "Whom do you see when you enter into communion with Jesus Christ?" That Christians do possess some sort of image of him in their minds, partially formed by the Scriptures, partially by liturgy, and partially by their own desires, whims and prejudices, becomes apparent when a "new" attempt to portray Jesus appears.

In 1920 Sir Jacob Epstein's first statue of Christ was exhibited for the first time at the Leicester Galleries in London and was greeted with horror and derision. A Roman Catholic priest wrote to the *Times*:

> I feel ready to cry out with indignation that in this Christian England there should be exhibited the figure of a Christ which suggested to me some degraded Chaldean or African, which wore the appearance of an Asiatic-American or Hun, which reminded me of some emaciated Hindu or badly grown Egyptian.[24]

Yet the Jewish sculptor had not set out to create a statue of Christ. Epstein was studying the head of his model Bernard Van Dieren, when he recognized in it the Christ head "with its short beard, its pitying accusing eyes, and the lofty and broad brow, denoting great intellectual strength." So he proceeded and the statue became the *Risen Christ*, his body swathed in clothes. He is standing up, the hands are large, imposing, the right hand with its flesh pierced, the wound open, held up for all to see, the left hand pointing to it. The head is a modern head, the brow intellectual, the nose fastidious, the mouth scornful, the eyes deep, accented, stylized. But it is the hands, the over life-size hands that matter, that capture and retain our attention.

Of this statue, widely reviled, occasionally acclaimed, Epstein wrote:

> How prophetic a figure! Not the early Evangelical Christ of Byzantium and Rome, not the condemning

Appollonian Christ of Michelangelo, or the sweet rising and blessing Christ of Raphael, but the modern living Christ, compassionate and accusing at the same time. I should like to remodel this "Christ." I should like to make it hundreds of feet high, and set it up on some high place where all could see it, and where it would give out its warning, its mighty symbolic warning to all lands. The Jew - the Galilean - condemns our wars, and warns us that "Shalom, Shalom," must be still the watchword between man and man.[25]

Looking back on this statue as he wrote his auto-biography, Epstein was satisfied and impressed with how well he had worked. "How in this work I realised the dignity of man, his feebleness, his strength, his humility, and the wrath and pity of the Son of Man."

It is true that there is a degree of secularization in Epstein's statue. The artist is seemingly interested in Christ as Man and as Prophet, accusing and condemning the world for its wars - its lust for war. But Epstein had some understanding of the meaning of the crucifixion, unlike another modern artist, Francis Bacon the painter, who used the crucifixion theme as a part of his non-religious conviction of the madness of this world and the inhumanity of human beings. Bacon's big *Crucifixion* triptych was painted under the continuous influence of alcohol. In it he attempted to make his own tragic feelings visual. Life is purposeless; there is no life after death, hell is here and now. This is what we see and feel in his triptych. What fascinates some critics is the extent to which Bacon is obsessed with the crucifixion event, but it can be suggested that he is merely drawn, as are many atheists, to the most dramatic incident in history, the great drama of human suffering, which says and shows more vividly than anything else what the artist wants most to say.

Epstein, too, was drawn to the drama surrounding Jesus Christ. As he worked he became more and more involved in the tradition concerning the person of Christ. In his *Majestas*, Epstein created an immense representation of Christ in Glory designed to hang upon a great cylinder containing the organ pipes in the restored medieval cathedral at Llandaff in Wales. Horton Davies has written of this statue:

> What is so astonishing about the *Majestas* is that it harmoniously combines three Christological concepts: the impassible Byzantine Christ enthroned in glory, the Semitic suffering Christ with sharp nose and agonising eyes, and the contemporary Christ whose hands plead *Shalom, Shalom*, to a world that does not know the secret of its peace.[26]

As one gazes at this figure, which seems to be floating, supernatural, and yet a contemporary person, attention is drawn to the hands. They are reaching out, not accusing or condemning this time, but reaching out in invitation, as if to say, come unto me all you who pass by and be partakers of my suffering and my glory.

There have been many other depictions of Christ by both Christians and non-Christians. I think of Graham Sutherland's *Crucifixion* at St. Aidan's Church, East Acton, London, which Horton and Hugh Davies see as "the complete opposite of common sentimental versions of the crucifixion in both the stark treatment and the color symbolism, with steel gray and crimson. The image is an austere symbol of the sheer costliness of sacrifice and, therefore, of the profound love of Christ, the crucified Redeemer."[27] Equally impressive is Sutherland's *Noli Me Tangere*, in Chichester Cathedral. In this painting, based on John 20:17, the risen Christ is depicted forbidding Mary Magdalen to touch him. It is apparent that the artist is a Christian, for there is a depth of understanding portrayed, especially in the figure of Christ. He forbids the Magdalen to touch him, but does it in such a way that he appears to be giving her a benediction. This is, after all, the woman who washed his feet and anointed them with precious oil, showing the vastness of her faith and dedication.

Georges Rouault focused attention upon the cross. He too was obsessed with the crucified Christ. The painter said: "As a Christian in such hazardous times, I believe only in Jesus on the Cross. I am a Christian of olden times." The cross is there in his famous *La Sainte Face* ("The Sacred Face"), the sad eyes with dark eyebrows above making, with the elongated nose, a cross in the face of Christ. This painting is marked, as are so many of Rouault's depictions, by compassion. It is through Christ's suffering and compassion that he is seen to be the Savior of all of those who suffer now. We know from looking at his paintings of the crucifixion how deeply Rouault sympathized with the victims of injustice, the poor and the lonely, the outcasts of this present world. He identifies that sympathy with Christ. Horton and Hugh Davies have this to say of Rouault:

No modern painter has so frequently depicted a Christ-centered faith or so consistently shown a Christ on the Cross in His total identification with human suffering and loneliness that He might make it endurable and eventually triumph over it. Bernard

Dorival has pointed out in his essay on "Rouault and Pascal" that the painter kept the *Pensées* on his bedside table and read and re-read them assiduously. In Rouault's paintings a three-fold theme is reiterated: it is the misery of man without God — the felicity of man with God — and a God that we only know through Jesus Christ. Francois Mauriac the novelist recognizes the scarlet thread of the tapestry of all Rouault's *oeuvre* from the dark paintings of the beginning to the hopeful and lyrical paintings at the end of his life was compassion.[28]

It is no wonder that Rouault's depictions of Christ have been so widely acclaimed by Christians who desire to avoid the sentimentality of many popular prints of Jesus Christ that adorn church vestibules and beauty parlors, yet want to see portrayed the divine compassion, as does Rouault's *Head of Christ* in the Chrysler Art Museum at Norfolk, Virginia.

The first necessity for the spiritual pilgrim is to put aside the illusion that there is an authoritative picture of Christ. Even if we had a photograph, it could not possibly present all that needs to be conveyed. Any painting, any statue, will be deficient. The second necessity is to take seriously the imaging of Christ in the mind, but to do so with reserve and humility. We have considered in Chapter 2 the use of the imagination in meditation. In meditation we might imagine the prophetic Christ, casting out the money changers from the Temple, as recorded in the New Testament, and protesting against war in this nuclear age, as we may conclude from our over-all understanding of the gospel that he would. Epstein's *Risen Christ* interprets this theme boldly. Imagine the compassionate Christ, whose compassion shows through his eyes, as in Rouault's *La Sainte Face*, the Son of God and Son of Man who suffers with those who suffer and weeps with those who weep. In him we know the compassion of God. And we know that God suffers with the dying people of Ethiopia and Chad and the Sudan. Imagine the Christ of glory, the Christ in triumph, risen from the dead, victorious over sin and death and meaninglessness. Joined together with him in faith, we can never fall into the abyss of nothingnesss. Although we die as all must die we shall not then come to an end, for in him we enter into eternal life, the life of glory.

We are taught in meditation to use our imaginations, and so we must do on our spiritual journeys - not only in imagining that is visual, at least to the mind's eye, but also in words (poetry is best suited to the task) and in music. The religious poet William Blake regarded imagination as integral to salvation, and this was so because he viewed the imagination as a religious faculty. Imagination is of critical importance to formal meditation, especially in the "composition of place;" according to the *Spiritual Exercises* of Ignatius of Loyola, we can come to see with the imagination some place, or person, or situation. In meditation upon the crucifixion, for example, we seek to see with the imagination the Christ on the cross. What we see there will in large part dictate the direction of the meditation. The Christian need not, in truth will not, see the same rendition each time. Given the richness of Jesus Christ in Scripture and in tradition we do not expect to see the same scene each time we look at the Christ on the cross.

What is it that we see? What is the inspiration for our seeing? We must venture through our imaginations, but we also need to be on guard. We may say, in accordance

[93]

with our beliefs, that it is the Holy Spirit that inspires us. But we also must test the spirits. How do we test the spirits? Chiefly we can test them through Scripture and tradition in the context of the church's worship. The senselessness of life that is conveyed by Francis Bacon's *Crucifixion* triptych would not be valid for one who took seriously the Johannine emphasis on Jesus as the life, the way, the truth. But one could imagine seeing what Graham Sutherland saw and painted in his *Noli Me Tangere*. Indeed, much of our imaging is inspired by the Scripture both read and interpreted in the liturgy. I think of Eucharistic Prayer A of Rite II in the *Book of Common Prayer*, which depicts the compassionate Christ:

> Holy and gracious Father: In your infinite love you made us for yourself; and, when we had fallen into sin and become subject to evil and death, you, in your mercy, sent Jesus Christ, your only and eternal Son, to share our human nature, to live and die as one of us, to reconcile us to you, the God and Father of all.
>
> He stretched out his arms upon the cross, and offered himself, in obedience to your will, a perfect sacrifice for the whole world.

The statement in words is simple, but the picture is immense and awesome. Georges Rouault's painting of Christ in the *Miserere* series, *Obedient unto Death, even the Death of the Cross*, captures the immensity and awesomeness of the scene. However, in my own mind there is a better portrayal - not in terms of artistic quality, but in terms of my own involvement. Through the eucharistic prayer I envision a suffering man transcending his finitude even as he experiences excruciating pain. He

[94]

is there not because he was trapped and put there, but because it was his vocation to be there, to stretch out his arms upon the cross, offering himself, the great High Priest himself the sacrifice, the Lamb of God, in obedience to his Father's will, a perfect sacrifice for the whole world, for everyone that is, that was, and that shall be, in all the cosmos, everywhere. He is there, his arms stretched out in surrender to God, his arms stretched out to embrace the world, everyone, everywhere, including me. In the end I find myself yielding to his call, sharing in his suffering, feeling the pangs of guilt and contrition, dying with him that I may be his, his alone, and rising with him to glory everlasting. What I see is no sweet, sickly, sentimental Jesus, but a Jesus who in his weakness and vulnerability displays strength beyond anything that I have known.

The imagination is not always active in the worship of the church, nor is it always engaged at the same place in the liturgy. There are times of dryness when our learning comes by way of deprivation. That to which I am referring is not something that happens with trumpets blaring in the midst of the Metro-Goldwyn-Mayer spectacular. What happens happens when I least expect it, and at times when I am so unprepared that it is only in retrospect that I understand that I have been present at an epiphany, an annunciation. The chief point is that I am engaged in the holy routine in such a way that I am not expecting or looking for something dramatic to titillate my spiritual senses and to show off to my friends some proof of my sanctity. Engaged in the holy routine of the church's corporate worship, not bogged down in preconceived notions of deity, sufficiently in awe of God and God's ways with me, I let my imagination play with the words and actions of the liturgy and am better able to enter into the sacred drama and be furthered in my spiritual journey through life in this world.

There is still another point,and one of considerable sensitivity. I have in mind the scene of the Great Judgment in Matthew 25, where Jesus confronts the righteous and the unrighteous with his assertion that in feeding the hungry, giving drink to those who thirst, welcoming the stranger, clothing the naked, and visiting the sick and those in prison, they are ministering to him. He says, "Truly, I say to you, as you did it to one of the least of these my brethren, you did it to me. . . . Truly, I say to you, as you did it not to one of the least of these, you did it not to me." Those who serve the needy inherit the kingdom and those who do not go away into eternal punishment. The scene is vivid and in itself subject-matter for meditation in which the imagination puts us in the picture. The Baptismal Covenant in the *Book of Common Prayer*, building on Matthew 25, asks, "Will you seek and serve Christ in all persons, loving your neighbor as yourself?" The people answer: "I will, with God's help."

With the conviction that no one image of Christ is going to suffice, it is possible to enlarge our understanding, as well as our communion, by looking at the starving child in Ethiopia and there seeing Christ, or by looking at the maimed survivor of Hiroshima and there seeing Christ, or by looking at the victim of apartheid in South Africa and there seeing Christ. The Christ we see suffering on the cross is identifying himself with all who suffer. We can see him, there, where a black child in Chicago is suffering from malnutrition, and where the battered wife in El Paso is pleading for a chance to start life over again. The power of such images is very great and capable of drawing us on into the bosom of God. To see Christ in such a way may involve us in ridicule and in suffering, but to deny Christ is not possible for those who live in communion with him.

Think back once more to the impact produced by Jacob Epstein's *Risen Christ*. The artist was faulted for depicting so human, so modern, so identifiable a figure and giving it such a sacred name. Yet this figure is convincing as a man, every man, and every woman who is suffering. As John Middleton Murray observed: "He is a man of sorrows and acquainted with grief. There is pain, bodily agony, not merely in the gesture with which he points to the torn flesh of his outspread hand, but in the poise of his proud unseeing head."[29] Here is one asking for, pleading for justice and mercy and deliverance, calling to us, as Epstein himself put it, to put an end to insane warfare. And here is Christ. There is a dreadful and powerful correspondence between the Christ of the cross and the Christ of suffering in this present world, the Christ present to us in those who experience agony, the victims of our madness. Look upon him and remember: "In as much as you did it not to one of the least of these, you did it not to me."

Edward Shillito, a priest, recognized the daring character of Epstein's *Risen Christ* and concluded:

> It must be admitted at once that this Christ would never make sense of the Gospel as a whole. No one could picture this Man taking children in His arms and sharing in feasts with publicans and sinners; the Christ of the Gospel was sharply distinguished from John the Baptist, the austere prophet. This Christ would have come like John. . . . This Christ would never have smiled or wept. Men would have feared and obeyed Him, and even died for Him; they would scarcely have loved Him.

Yet there is another figure in the Gospel, and the value of this great work lies in the insight which has led the artist to interpret this other strand in the story. This may have been the Christ of whom men said: "Elijah is returned." This may have been the Christ who strode ahead of His disciples towards the city, and they were afraid of Him . . . .[30]

So it shall be with our pictures of Christ. They shall none of them be complete, but all of them, to the degree that they are in tune with the Scriptures and tradition, will be important for us on our spiritual journeys. Furthermore, one depiction of Christ may at one time appear one way and at another time another way, just as Middleton Murray could look at the *Risen Christ* and see the man of suffering representing the suffering of the world and Edward Shillito could look at the same statue and see the Christ of whom it was said, "Elijah is returned."

The one with whom we enter into fellowship, with whom we are united, is Christ the Lord, whom we see in a diversity of ways in varying circumstances. We may be assured that he is a person who is related to us in personal ways. It is with this assurance that we can speak of spirituality as communion, beginning with God as revealed in Jesus Christ.

Christian Spirituality and Modern Humanity

The condition of humanity in this twentieth century is reflected in the ways that Jesus Christ is depicted in this era. As we have seen, the most impressive sculptures and paintings of Christ have emphasized the prophetic

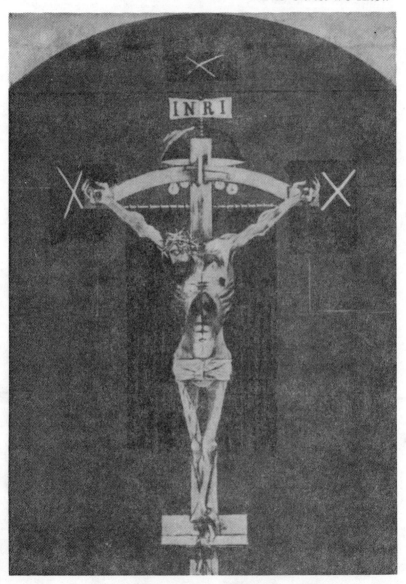

Graham Sutherland, <u>Crucifixion</u>

Jacob Epstein, <u>Christ in Majesty</u>

Christ in Majesty (detail)

Graham Sutherland, <u>Noli me tangere</u>

Georges Rouault, <u>Obedient Unto Death, Even the Death of the Cross</u>

Georges Rouault, <u>La Sainte Face</u>

Georges Rouault, <u>Christ in the Suburbs</u>

Georges Rouault, <u>Street of the Lonely</u>

Christ and the compassionate Christ. The prophetic points to and condemns the inhumanity of this age, its disregard for God and God's laws. The prophecy contains the warning that unless there is radical change in the heart and in the behavior of humanity, wholesale destruction and utter doom shall ensue. The compassionate Christ reaches out in love and pity to those who are deprived and oppressed. Georges Rouault, in his *Miserere* series, emphasized the miseries of the poor and the concern of Christ who is with the poor in their sufferings. In *The Hard Business of Living* Rouault depicts a man weary and worn, his head bent as if he felt the weight of the world upon him. In his face there is an expression of grief passing into death. This is not the man of great affairs, the entrepreneur, the head of state. This is one who knows how difficult, how painful it is to live day to day.

The Hard Business of Living is not all that Rouault has to depict. In *Christ in the Suburbs*, he pictures a dark street of shadows, uninviting doorways, windows too small to allow very much daylight to penetrate the unseen interiors, and a lowering, dark sky. But then, one's attention is called to the bright sun, penetrating the dark sky, illuminating the dismal industrial suburbs of Paris, falling upon a figure — the figure of Christ in the foreground, Christ for whom the sun is a halo, standing in the otherwise deserted street with two children, lonely and solemn. The scene is drab and ominous, but in its midst there is a glimmer of hope. Christ is there with the children. It is possible, meditating upon this scene, to hear Christ crying out against the injustice and inhumanity of the modern, industrial city — weeping over this Paris — and saying with prophetic emphasis, "Blessed are you poor, for yours is the Kingdom of God . . . But

woe to you that are rich, for you have received your con-
solation."

Rouault's depiction of the drabness and harshness of
his world is unrelenting. In another picture in the
Miserere series we see a house receding into the back-
ground on one side of the street and on the other side a
factory or a warehouse, cold and blank. This is *The
Street of the Lonely*, reminding us of the heartlessness
and loneliness of life in our modern, industrialized
society. There are other etchings, one of a rather lifeless
looking woman, called *The Society Lady fancies she has a
reserved seat in heaven*, and another, a caricature, showing
what I imagine to be a modern business man dressed as a
king, called *We think ourselves kings*. In these the artist
expresses something of the pretension and futility of
modern society. Other etchings depict skeletons rising
out of their graves led by one wearing a soldier's cap, and
skulls arranged in rows in a church crypt. Both etchings
bear titles concerned with resurrection: *He that believeth
in me, though he were dead, yet shall he live* and *Dead
man, arise!* We may believe, but for the moment, chill
death surrounds us and the only word that we can utter is
miserere. It is no longer possible to distinguish between
times of war and times of peace. Times of peace are not
without their wars, and if somewhere there is no actual
war there are still preparations for war, so our lives are
lived in memory of the last war and in anticipation of the
next.

There are other ways of looking at contemporary
society. T. S. Eliot has accustomed many of us to recognize the superficiality of much of modern life. We have
met hollow men and women; we have listened to the twittering of aunts and uncles, discussing the younger generation and its dreadful habits, its cigarettes and cocktails;

we have stood crowded in a mass of humanity on subway trains and in elevators, pressed close to one another and yet not seeing and certainly not feeling the other. I am haunted by the picture of the typist in T. S. Eliot's *The Waste Land*, arriving home, letting in a young man, a sailor who is home from sea, allowing him to copulate with her and sending him on his way with a meaningless kiss. When he has gone she quickly forgets, relieved that it is over, adjusts her hair, and puts a record on the record player. This indifference is worse than the twittering, and yet perhaps it amounts to the same thing, a way of avoiding that which we cannot or will not face: death and destruction. We are reminded of Walker Percy's characters, Binx Bolling and Thomas More, who suffer from boredom, ennui, or, as Eliot might say "acedia" or the "aboulie" that he spoke of as a kind of life-long affliction, a sense of dread-loss. One feels what is meant in Binx Bolling's lines in *The Moviegoer* as he answers Aunt Emily's probing questions:

> "Don't you feel obliged to use your brain and to make a contribution?"
> "No'm."
> "Don't you love these things? Don't you live by them?"
> "No."
> "What do you love? What do you live by?"
> I am silent.[31]

Life in the modern world is debilitating for many people. Of the many moral ills that plague us, one of the most serious is a growing insensitivity toward anything beyond the isolated self. The consumer-oriented, hi-tech society in which we live urges us to be more and more centered upon self and self-satisfaction, with the promise of more luxuries to come. The risk of nuclear war is overshadowed by the spin-offs of space-age technology that provide better health care and more comforts for us, "as individuals," so we say. If we have lost the ability to perceive the reality beyond the appearances, if we suffer from spiritual entropy, that is, after all, a small price to pay for all the benefits we have that our grandparents never dreamed of having. So why bother about making a contribution to benefit our children and our children's children? It is the now that matters. Why be concerned if you cannot identify anything as loved or worth living for, when you are enjoying the moment?

As we have seen, however, human beings do in fact need something beyond that which they possess as creatures in a technological heaven (or hell). They need relationships that matter, relationships on which they can count. They need to develop as human beings and thus they need to be able to give for the good of others as well as to receive. They need to receive with thanksgiving, and without suspicion and the burden of belief that they must repay those who give to them. They need to be in communion with the Ultimate. And so they set about to satisfy all of these needs. We have referred to the predominant religiosity of Americans as individual and private; they are consumers choosing from a wide range of options, those things that will best serve their own religious and psychological needs. Living in a technological society, we become entranced with the technology of religion.

William Barrett, writing of our ambivalence toward technology, speaks to the contemporary situation when he points to the fact that complain as much as we do about all the hardware of technology, we secretly nourish a fascination with technique itself. The publishing market is regularly flooded with "how to" manuals of all kinds. We turn to books to learn how to make love, and in consequence sex comes to be thought of as mainly a technique. Treatises on mental health appear that carry with them their own built-in little self-help kit of psychotherapy. All of this would be comic if it weren't also so pathetic — and ultimately dangerous. This worship of technique is in fact more childish than the worship of machines. You have only to find the right method, the definite procedure, and all problems in life must inevitably yield before it.[32]

Multitudes of moderns are far more interested in religious technique than they are in the God made manifest in Jesus Christ through the activity of the Holy Spirit. Furthermore, these same people look to books and courses on spirituality to provide them with techniques which will tell in simple, clear words how to pray, how to meditate, how to have a fuller and richer life, or how to be assured of immortality.

It is not surprising that in a society such as ours there is a crisis of identity, a sense of worthlessness amongst so many, and a worship of celebrities — with whom one can feel some sense of kinship without the risk of intimacy. But the most alluring religion for such a time as ours is dualistic: the all-righteous nation pitted against the evil, satanic empire of the enemy. Somehow such an idolatry provides meaning and a sense of righteousness that we can seemingly find nowhere else. When reminded of the risks involved in escalating tensions between superpowers, we are inclined either to see the choice as one between escalation and surrender, or else we may evade the issue and seek to shut out of our minds what might interfere with our pursuit of the satisfaction of the moment.

That there is much good in our contemporary world cannot be denied. There are many who dedicate their lives to making this world a more humane place to live, a place in which the quality of relationships is more highly valued than the quantity of things possessed. There are those genuinely committed to the pursuit of peace, not only for our nation, but for all nations. There are many whole-heartedly committed to communion with God in Christ Jesus through the activity of the Holy Spirit. In 1977 Janani Luwum, the Archbishop of Uganda, spoke out for justice and the rule of law in East Africa where the despot Idi Amin ruled as a law unto himself. Luwum was seized, tried, beaten and shot to death by Amin and his army. The archbishop died confidently confessing faith in Jesus Christ. People pray and the sick are healed by faith through the activity of the Holy Spirit. There are holy places where Christ's presence has been known and prayer has risen like incense in the evening and the sacrifice once for all upon the cross has been powerful in changing people's lives.

Let the prophets of doom beware; there are forces abroad in this twentieth century determined to disprove the grim prophecies. We must not forget that although in so many ways Western technology is dominant in our world, it has its challengers in the Third World and among the great founded, world religions. Furthermore, Western technology produces the instruments of its own self-criticism. Of great importance in this regard is the revolution in communications, including the advent of communications satellites in space, which makes it progressively more difficult for the manipulators of technology to do anything without all the world knowing what is happening. Our high-tech communications networks keep us in touch with suffering in Lebanon and Ethiopia, in Afghanistan and Appalachia. Other technological advances increase our ability to respond to people in need and thus to serve Christ in our neighbors.

For Christians there is the conviction, based upon the witness of Scripture and tradition, reason and revelation, that God is no absentee landlord, but is presently active in the created order. Our need for communion, which is ultimately communion not only with other persons but with God in Christ Jesus, disturbs us, makes us restless, and arouses us to reach out beyond ourselves to others and to God. The Holy Spirit is active in the midst of people, preeminently in the midst of God's chosen people, Christ's body, the church, to lift high the cross of Christ, enabling agents of Christ's sacrifical love and service, that Christ may draw all people to communion with himself, uniting them with one another in a common commitment to mutual participation and mutual care and love.

Christians are never perfect, although they radiate that perfection which is the wholeness they have with one another in Christ. They are, as we have said, echoing Luther, *simul justus et peccator*, but they are in Christ as he is in them, being sanctified through the working of God's Spirit in and through word and sacrament in the holy fellowship. Christians are by nature realists and at the same time optimists. They are realists in their assessment of the world condition, but they are optimists in their conviction that God has already won the battle for the salvation of his people and his creation. God has won it in and through Jesus Christ. This does not mean that we shall survive according to the world's understanding of survival. But it does mean that we shall have eternal life, for we have already entered into that life in Christ.

Rouault's *Miserere* etchings condemn the world for its inhumanity, its sinfulness, its cruelty, but as we have observed, the artist's entire life was given over to the theme of death and resurrection. Horton and Hugh Davies note that the *Miserere* "is the most completely religious of all Rouault's works, for it interprets human destiny in terms of fallen man's rescue by the compassion of Christ." There are hints of resurrection in Rouault's grim portrayal of the resurrection of the dead, in his depiction of two children on a suburban street with its factories and warehouses which are like threatening monsters. Christ is shown with the children, accompanying them in their grim habitat. The final plates of the *Miserere* series emphasize the hope that was in the artist and his Roman Catholic faith. Depicting the Virgin with the child in her arms, one has the title *In these dark times of vainglory and unbelief, Our Lady of Land's End keeps vigil*. The last plate shows the thorn-crowned head of Christ imprinted on Veronica's veil. Its title is *And with His stripes we are healed*. Rouault's message seems to be that as Christ went the way of the cross so he will accompany us as we go through the darkness of our times, caring for us with compassion, leading us in the way of sacrificial love and service until we all come to that kingdom which he has prepared for us, triumphant over death and sin and meaninglessness.

Some may say that there has never been a darker time than this time in which we live. The artist Robert Morris in his *Fire Storm* series depicts the firestorm that destroyed Hiroshima and will destroy anything and everything that is exposed to the horrors of the nuclear blast.[33] His inspiration is Leonardo da Vinci's *Deluge* drawings of the Old Testament account of the great flood that covered the earth. We live with the threat of nuclear holocaust ever present with us. There is no denying the darkness of the times, but for those who live in communion with Christ, no matter how fragile that communion may be and no matter how beseiged with doubts the disciple may be, the terrifying possibility of nuclear holocaust is not the last word. God has the last word, and that word is Christ. That word is the law that rules and shall forever rule the universe, the law of sacrifice. Knowing that God has the last word makes it possible for Christians to acknowledge reality and to work in the fellowship of the Holy Spirit to turn people, to be God's agents for *metanoia* (repentance), that God's will may be done in earth as it is in heaven.

Between God and the Christian: The Holy Spirit
and Prayer

In our time of doubt and skepticism concerning theological and spiritual matters, the idea of the Holy Spirit is problematic at best. It is a problem that has forced theologians to seek for explanations convincing enough to lead people to the threshold of faith. Such explanations, if they are to be effective, combine traditional understandings with contemporary ways of thinking. One way of explaining the meaning of the doctrine of the Holy Spirit has been basic to the argument of this book.

Spirituality concerns communion, communion between the object of our faith, God in Christ Jesus, and ourselves, twentieth-century humans. Between Christ and ourselves there is a current of communication, such as has been described when considering the participant, as distinguished from the spectator. This communion can be compared to the communion between two people in which an unspoken communication takes place. John Donne, in his poem "The Extasie," speaks of this in terms of a man and woman in love. In the twentieth century the Scottish poet Edwin Muir describes the same sense of communion and communication, not between two human beings, but between the Angel Gabriel and the Virgin Mary. That poem is "The Annunciation":

> . . . See, they have come together, see,
> While the destroying minutes flow,
> Each reflects the other's face
> Till heaven in hers and earth in his
> Shine steady there. He's come to her
> From far beyond the farthest star,
> Feathered through time. Immediacy
> Of strangest strangeness is the bliss
> That from their limbs all movement takes.
> Yet the increasing rapture brings
> So great a wonder that it makes
> Each feather tremble on his wings. . . .
> But through the endless afternoon
> These neither speak nor movement make,
> But stare into their deepening trance
> As if their gaze would never break.[34]

W. H. Auden's Mary in, "For the Time Being" seems to be more like one of us, for she does not "see" Gabriel. Rather she "feels" the currents of communication rushing through her body, causing her to say:

> What dancing joy would whirl
> My ignorance away

Light blazes out of the stone,
The taciturn water
Burst into music,
And warm wings throb within
The motionless rose:
What sudden rush of Power
Commands me to command?[35]

John V. Taylor, the retired Bishop of Winchester, speaks about such annunciations in a way that is reminiscent of T. S. Eliot in *Four Quartets*. We are made ready for communion with God by means of our experience of communion with people and things on the ordinary level of day-to-day experience. Of course we may not be sensitive to their happening, but if we are open to the possibility and are ready to receive communications from beyond ourselves, we may know something of the deepest meaning of beauty when we encounter the first spring flower. We may receive communications of caring love from our children and know the deepest joy of parenthood. Taylor directs our attention to the "current of communication" between I and Thou. Christians, he tells us,

> find it quite natural to give a personal name to this current of communication, this invisible go-between. They call him the Holy Spirit, the Spirit of God. They say that this was the Spirit which possessed and dominated the man Jesus Christ, making him the most aware and sensitive and open human being who has ever lived - ceaselessly aware of God so that he called him, almost casually, Father, and fantastically aware of every person who crossed his path, especially the ones no one else noticed.

[117]

That is the Spirit which he promised to his friends and on the day of Pentecost that is the Spirit which came and possessed them just as he had possessed Jesus. And what was the first immediate result of his coming? - Communication. Awareness.[36]

Two points require emphasis here. The first is that for Christians the communion, communication, and awareness which occur in day-to-day experiences between people and between people and things — paintings, music, flowers, and so on — are the work of the Holy Spirit. How do we know that it is the work of the Holy Spirit and not some other, possibly evil, spirit? By testing the spirits. One thing we know is that the Holy Spirit is the Spirit of God and thus the Spirit of Christ. We can rest assured, although not without doubt - we never escape altogether from doubt - that the working of the Holy Spirit will never run counter to what we know in Scripture and in tradition, of Jesus Christ. Further, we must ask whether what we are inclined to identify with the activity of the Spirit is in accord with the fruits of the Spirit (1 Cor. 13; Gal. 5:16-23). Above all, the work of the Spirit is *agapé*, love, love of God and love of neighbor, love that is unselfish and sacrificial. But once that warning is heeded, the Christian is at liberty to identify the activity of the Holy Spirit with seemingly ordinary occasions and events. Taylor also calls the Holy Spirit "that power which opens eyes that are closed, hearts that are unaware and minds that shrink from too much reality." He would identify the work of the Spirit not only with the communion, communication, and awareness, but also with the initiation of this work. Such an initiation Taylor does not limit to the opening of the eyes toward "the beauty of the world," and "the truth of ideas," but also to "the pain of disappointment and deformity." He concludes: "If one is closed up against being hurt, or blind toward one's fellow-men, one is inevitably shut off from God also. One cannot choose to be open in one direction and closed in another. Vision and vulnerability go together. Insensitivity also is an all-rounder. If for one reason or another we refuse really to *see* another person, we become incapable of sensing the presence of God."[37]

The second point requiring emphasis here concerns the tendency on the part of many people to identify strong appreciation of the doctrine of the Holy Spirit with renewal and charismatic movements. Pentecostalism and the charismatic movement tend to emphasize baptism in the Spirit either following conversion or at the time of conversion. Whatever the specifics of their belief, the pentecostal churches and the charismatic movement in Roman Catholic and mainline Protestant churches emphasize (some would say over-emphasize) the doctrine of the Holy Spirit as it is understood in the New Testament. Perhaps we had better say instead that the pentecostals, classical and new, are emphasizing a doctrine that too long has been neglected by the mainline churches. To say this does not mean we agree with everything they teach and everything they do, but that their over-emphasis on something essential and right calls our attention to our own neglect. The pentecostals are calling the churches back to the fullness of the Triune faith.

The Holy Spirit as communion, communication, and awareness, the Spirit of God curing our blindness so that we can "see" God and be aware of God's activity amongst us, is a lively reality in our experiences, both ordinary and extraordinary. The recovery of this understanding is of importance to twentieth-century seekers and it is comparable to the faith once delivered to the saints. Richard Hooker imagined prayer as consisting of angels descending with doctrine and angels ascending with prayer. We can now say that our communion with God begins with the Holy Spirit descending upon us and into us to open our eyes to see God and our neighbors and all of creation in a new and truer way. The Holy Spirit is, to use Bishop Taylor's way of putting it, the "go-between" God who creates saving fellowship with God and with one another in God. "What *causes* the fellowship is the gift of awareness which opens our eyes to one another, makes us see as we never saw before, the secret of all evolution, the spark that sets off most revolution, the dangerous life-giver, the Holy Spirit."[38]

Prayer is the response we make to the gift of awareness that we receive from God through the activity of the Holy Spirit. Since prayer is a part, and a necessary part, of the communion we have with God, it is also the work of the Holy Spirit. The Spirit is in the very breath of prayer, prayer which is, as Herbert taught, God's breath returning to its source. We have noted that prayer is far more than *prayers*. This distinction is understandable when we consider prayer as the human response to God's initiative in bringing into being a saving relationship, or when we think of prayer as God's breath returning to its source.

In our contemporary society, where relationship with God is so often related to prayer, and prayer is a matter of formal prayers or of extempore prayer which possesses a certain formality, spirituality seems to be a formidable task. The common experience of those who seek this relationship is one of frustration. They are determined to pray regularly, and then they are not able to do so; they adopt a rule of regular prayer and then find that twentieth-century life seems not to allow the keeping of such a rule. Furthermore, there is the question of whether or not we are heard when we pray, and the question as to whether or not there is anyone there to hear.

It is necessary to consider all the different meanings of prayer and to come to an understanding that does justice both to tradition and to the conditions in which we live. John Macquarrie argues that

> prayer is a fundamental style of thinking, passionate and compassionate, responsible and thankful, that is deeply rooted in our humanity and that manifests itself not only among believers but also among serious-minded people who do not possess any religious faith. Yet it seems to me that if we follow out the instinct to pray that is in all of us, it will finally bring us to faith in God.[39]

In truth there are many people who chastise themselves for not praying when in fact they are engaged in prayer; they are responsive to the working of the Holy Spirit in their midst, arousing in them passionate, compassionate, responsible, and thankful thinking. Indeed, we can rightly speak of prayer in essence as becoming a *"conscious relationship* between man and God, whether or not that relationship is recognised or articulated," as Martin Thornton writes, building on John Macquarrie's theology.

To be in relationship with God is to be at prayer. Our relationship with God involves the descent and ascent of angels, the Holy Spirit coming into our lives to open our eyes to God's work and will for the world and our response, through the agency of the Holy Spirit, which response is prayer. Prayer is not an isolated experience, but a living relationship. Specific prayers, both corporate and private, constitute points of focus or concentrates in the midst of that continuous relationship. Martin Thornton argues that

> once we reverse the Benedictine order and see habitual relationship with God as primary prayer, and acts - saying prayers - as secondary, then we are back to the values of the primitive age, and we have simplified things enormously. If prayer is relationship with God and acts of prayer - or periods of prayer or just prayers - are foci or concentrates of it, then it is obvious that prayer and life are the same thing. If an act of prayer, in church, or in private, or even a long period of solitary silence, is an articulated concentrate of faith-experience, then it cannot be misunderstood as withdrawal, or escape, from life.[40]

To engage in acts of prayer, whether private or corporate, is to enter more deeply into life, for life is relationship and communion with God.

What is being emphasized here is something that John Taylor put quite simply by saying, "To live in Christ is to live in prayer. Prayer is not something you do; it is a style of living. It is living under the witness which the Spirit bears with our spirits that we are the sons of God." Prayer, in the secondary sense of "saying prayers," can be understood in its most rudimentary form in terms of our sudden awareness of something or someone deeply cherished. It is then an expression of gratitude, sheer joy for the gift that is the flower or the friend. That sense of gratitude or joy is prolonged in prayer, savored, and allowed to have its good effect. Then, too, as Taylor also suggests, prayer may be awareness of need - "God help me" - or it may be an expression of weariness - "God, I'm tired." Conscious prayer takes such spontaneous expressions and draws them out, offering the reality in them to God. Personal devotions can quite helpfully be based upon recollections of such incidents of awareness during the day. Then there is the reaction that occurs when we realize that someone is in pain or need of any kind. "God help him," we say, and thus make a prayer of intercession; in the middle of it we may become aware of some way in which we can help the person for whom we pray. Finally there is the prayer of repentance, perhaps when we have done something that we thought right and have come to realize that it was all wrong. Then comes the prayer of contrition, "God, I wish I hadn't done that. I'm sorry, I feel rotten about it."[41]

Having arrived this far, we can remind ourselves of what the church has considered the standard forms of prayer. There is the prayer of adoration, which for the mystics is the contemplation of God as God is in himself, and for most of us is an act of love and praise as we contemplate what God has done for us. The contemplation of God issues in confession, the acknowledgment of our failures, personal and social, in relation to God and our neighbors. Confession is a bowing down, an abasement of oneself in contrition before our righteous, merciful God. After confessing our sins and receiving forgiveness, we make bold to offer our petitions and intercessions. Lancelot Andrewes taught that the prayer of petition is not pretentious since Christ commands that we pray thus and gave us a form of prayer, the Lord's Prayer, as an example. Furthermore, Andrewes cited John 16:23, "Whatsoever you ask My Father in My Name, He will give it to you." But we must take care, for prayers of petition and intercession, in which we ask God to act on our behalf or on behalf of others for whom we are concerned, must be done in the context of adoration and confession - in the atmosphere and in the midst of our relationship with God. Finally, there are prayers of praise and thanksgiving. Praise is the outward expression of our communion with God in words, in music, in ceremonial acts, focused on what God has done for us and principally for the Word made flesh, sacrificed for us. Thanksgiving is closely linked to praise, as in the General Thanksgiving of the Prayer Book.

These are some of the traditional forms of prayer, but I would emphasize that in essence prayer is communion with God, communion that extends beyond itself into relationships with others. Thus prayer can be and often is the prayer of silence. To be silent is to turn inward towards "the still point of the turning world," toward the divine presence at the heart of being. This positive silence is an enjoying of the divine and becomes prayer when and as God fills the emptiness. Meister Eckhart wrote, "Here he [i.e., the person] meets God without intermediary. And from out of the Divine Unity there shines into him a simple light: and this light shows him Darkness and Nakedness, and Nothingness."

Beyond the silence there are words. There need not be many words. In the Eastern Church, the Jesus Prayer has been used to promote "hesychasm" (*hesuchia*, silence), a state of perpetual prayerfulness. It is a simple prayer: "Lord Jesus Christ, Son of God, have mercy on me, a sinner." The prayer can be reduced to the simple repetition of the name of Jesus, and it can fade into silence. The words that issue from silence and cultivate the life of prayer can, in fact, be any words at all, the communication of the faithful with the source of all life-giving, saving communication.

One further thought concerns the possibility that when considering prayer we should take into account the fruits of prayer, the words and deeds of love resulting from prayer as conscious relationship with God. That relationship with God extends into relationships with others and effects the quality of our living in relationship, in community. Thomas Merton, the Trappist monk, believed, for instance, that prayer was linked to the awakening of the social conscience. The spiritual life, including prayer, involves the whole life of the whole person. Writing of Merton, Kenneth Leech states that "the understanding of prayer is crucial to the understanding of social change. There is no split between spirituality and social responsibility. He sees prayer as 'a consciousness of man's union with God' and 'an awareness of one's inner self.'"[42] Such consciousness, such awareness, is transforming. It drives those who are engaged in the life of prayer beyond the destructive tendencies of individualism in Western politics and theology to the creative fruits of communion with God that includes communion, caring and sacrificial relationships with others.

In the end, our considerations of the Holy Spirit and of prayer are of one piece, for they both concern our relationship with God. The Holy Spirit is active in the in-betweenness of ourselves and God in Christ, opening our eyes to knowledge of God as found in the Book of Scripture and the Book of Creatures and stirring our minds to passionate, compassionate, responsible, thankful thinking, in and through corporate worship and in private devotions. From this perspective we can say with the ancients that prayer is a "sharing of the divine nature"; in the words of Gregory of Sinai, "Prayer is God."[43] Julian of Norwich, the fourteenth-century English anchoress, believed that prayer uniting us to God "is a right understanding of that fulness of joy which is to come, with true longing and thirst." In her fourteenth revelation, Julian writes,

> When our courteous Lord of his special grace shows himself to our soul, we have what we desire, and then for that time we do not see what more we should pray for, but all our intentions and all our powers are wholly directed to contemplating him. And as I see it, this is an exalted and imperceptible prayer; for the whole reason why we pray is to be united into the vision and contemplation of him to whom we pray, wonderfully rejoicing with reverent fear, and with so much sweetness and delight in him that we cannot pray at all except as he moves us at the time.[44]

The Church as Context for Spirituality

Moderns sometimes are baffled altogether when they try to understand what it means to be in communion with Christ, he in them and they in him. They may try to think of some "spiritual" experience whereby they as individuals transcend all human limits to ascend to the Risen Christ and there, wherever it may be, enter into fellowship. That this way of thinking is common should not be surprising. Spirituality must involve ecclesiology, but this view is not commonly held. Yet through the ages Christians have understood that to be in Christ is to be in the church, and conversely to be in the church is to be in

Christ. We are baptized into the name of Jesus Christ *and* received into the church in the sacrament of Holy Baptism. The context in which spirituality normally exists and grows, is the church. So we may say that to be in communion with Christ, he in us and we in him, is to be members of a church which was, after all, brought into being by God operating through the Holy Spirit.

One of the ways the church has been understood from New Testament times through the years was strongly promoted by St. Paul. He called the church the body of Christ (Col. 1:24, Eph. 1:22). As though anticipating the problems in too close an identification of the earthly, fallible, finite church with Jesus Christ, Paul also spoke of Christ as the *head* of the body (Col. 1:18, Eph. 5:23). The church, the body of Christ, is thus subordinate to Christ, its head. The church is not to be thought of as Christ in any literal or absolute sense. It is Christ's body as his beloved possession; thus his body must live under the direction of and in obedience to its head. Nevertheless, since it is comprised of those saved by him, who are recipients of his grace and imbued with his Spirit and participate in his resurrection, it is altogether appropriate to speak of the church as the body of Christ. For these people, as the body, are the instrument of his living presence, his ever-active grace in and for the world. Christ's mission and ministry continue in and through the church, his body.

Paul's image also concerns the union and the mutual, caring interdependence of the members of the body. Paul said to the Romans, "We, though many, are one body in Christ, and individually members one of another" (Rom. 12:5; see 1 Cor. 12:27). Here the oneness of the members is emphasized, in spite of their diversity, but we may also conclude that the individuality of the members is impor-

[127]

tant. Those who comprise the church are many, and yet one body; one body, and yet individually members of it and of one another. The members exercise different ministries, grace being given to each "according to the measure of Christ's gift" (Eph. 4:7). According to this understanding, the church is the people of God and composed of diverse persons engaged in a great variety of ministries. The people are at one and the same time individuals and yet joined together in one body. This understanding of the church is more organic than sociological. The conjunction of widely differing persons in the one Christ, thereby becomes one body.

Ultimately the emphasis falls upon oneness in Christ. The conjunction being *in* Christ — all members being related both individually and corporately to Christ — suggests that we may also regard the church as the community of disciples, those who follow Christ in his ministry and mission. This body is then known as the servant church, a people participating in Christ's ministry of sacrificial love and service. The church also may be called the sacrament of Christ. Henri de Lubac has written:

> If Christ is the sacrament of God, the Church is for us the sacrament of Christ; she represents him, in the full and ancient meaning of the term, she really makes him present. She not only carries on his work, but she is his very continuation, in a sense more real than that in which it can be said that any human institution is its founder's continuation.[45]

Three matters require further emphasis if we are to try to understand the church as the context for spirituality. The first concerns the corporate nature of the church. Any thorough-going understanding of this corporate nature depends upon an understanding of wholeness incorporating lesser units, including individuals. We should remember that "strong support is found in I Cor. i, 2 and II Cor. i, 1 for the contention that the Church is not a great community made up of an accumulation of small communities, but is truly present in its wholeness in every company of believers, however small."[46] The wholeness of the church, the church triumphant in heaven and the church on earth, is manifest - or should be manifest - in each local gathering of Christians, no matter how insignificant the gathering may seem when judged by worldly standards. The church is always the entire body of Christ, however small the unit may be. Indeed, as Karl Schmidt the biblical critic says, "the one essential is communion with Christ. To put the matter in a nutshell - a single individual could be - would have to be - the *ecclesia* if he has communion with Christ. This is the basis of true human brotherhood."[47] Schmidt's point is logical and, as such, is convincing. One can imagine the circumstance where an individual Christian is isolated and alone. Such a person needs to know that she is not alone, but rather that the entire church by virtue of common participation in Christ, is where she is. Normally, however, our communion with Christ involves communion with other members of his body. We as individuals are conjoined in Christ, whose body we are: we are each of us in communion with Christ, "the temple of the living God" (2 Cor. 6:16). At the same time the church is God's temple, as we see in 1 Cor. 3:16 and 6:19. In the former passage, as C. K. Barrett notes, "Paul thinks of a corporate rather than an individual indwelling, though 'God can only dwell in the midst by indwelling in each one' (Calvin)."[48]

[129]

The second matter requiring further consideration is the importance of worship to the church as the body of Christ. This of course emphasizes the corporate worship of the church. In our society the tendency is to consider our corporate worship in terms of what we as individuals may gain from it. This is perfectly natural, but altogether wrong. What we need instead is an appreciation of corporate worship as far more important than anything we may gain, including our personal salvation. Evelyn Underhill makes this point, concluding that the corporate life of worship "stands for the total orientation of life toward God; expressed both through stylized liturgical action, and spontaneous common praise." Further on, she says that the

> total liturgical life of the *Corpus Christi* is not merely a collection of services, offices, and sacraments. Deeply considered, it is the sacrificial life of Christ Himself; the Word indwelling His Church, gathering in His eternal priestly action the small Godward movements, sacrifices, and aspirations of 'all the broken and the meek', and acting through those ordered signs and sacraments by means of these His members on earth.[49]

The operative principal, no matter what the characteristic style of particular denominations may be, remains the same: "the eternal self-offering of Christ to God in and through this mystical body." Yet the assembling of the individuals who believe the same things is not all that there is to the corporate worship of the church. That worship, argues Underhill,

> is real in its own right; an action transcending and

embracing all the seperate souls taking part in it. The individual as such dies to his seperate selfhood - even his spiritual selfhood - on entering the Divine Society: is 'buried in baptism' and reborn as a living cell of the Mystical Body of Christ. St Paul insists again and again on this transfer of status as the essential point of Christianity [Eph. 1:22, 23; 2:19-22; Col. 2:10, 13; 3:1-3,etc.]. Therefore the response to God of this whole Body, this supernatural organism, in life and in worshipping acts, is of cardinal importance; and since this response is to take place on earth as in heaven, it must have its here-and-now embodiment - inadequate as this must always be to the supernatural situation it shows forth.[50]

The church at worship, as faulty as it may be in the doing of the liturgy, is most fully what it is meant to be: the living, acting body of Christ. Liturgy not only brings before God those concerns that the community has as a corporate whole, it enables participation in the sacrifice that is at the heart of the universe and of all ultimate meaning. Then and there, in word and sacrament, in communion with God in Christ, the church confesses its sins, opens up to receive the Word, and enters into Christ's sacrifice - offering up its communal life, souls and bodies, "to be a reasonable, holy, and living sacrifice" unto God. In and through the body of Christ, Christ's saving presence and the sacrifice on the cross are made known and effective in and for the world. The challenge for the individuals composing the body is to realize what is the corporate worship of the church. In worship the members of the body together receive word and sacrament and respond with prayer; worship is not some spiritual deposit from which we may obtain whatever we find to be useful or beneficial to ourselves as individuals. R. K. Orchard wrote the following sentences about Christian mission; let me suggest that it is appropriate to substitute "worship" for "mission," with the understanding that worship issues in mission and that mission issues in worship:

> To share in Christ's mission is to join the whole choir of heaven in adoration of His Father and our Father, His God and our God. It is to share by faith in His ascension. It is to join in a doxology, sung by the first representatives of a new humanity, that all mankind may join in the praise of God which is the true meaning of its existence.[51]

To worship in the church is to participate in Christ's worship of the Father. This understanding is especially difficult to grasp in a time when there has been much strife, some of it bitter, leading to a revised liturgy, but it is vital that this understanding be grasped no matter how difficult.

The third point demanding further emphasis is the concept that to be in Christ is to be in the church, and to be in the church is to be in Christ. For those who have difficulty imagining what it means to "be in Christ," when considered solely on an individual basis, it must come as something of a relief to discover that as baptized members of the church we already are in Christ and he is in us. Christian mysticism need not be obscurantist. To enter into a deeper communion with Christ is to realize more and more fully an objective truth: we are in Christ and he is in us by virtue of our membership in his body. To enter more and more deeply into that communion, which is to develop a more telling and effective spirituality, is to be what we are, members of Christ's body. And to become so increasingly more deeply is to give up ourselves more and more fully to the worship of God in Christ through the activity of the Holy Spirit. It is to enter more and more into Christ's mission and ministry of sacrificial love and service, becoming agents for the restoration of all people to unity with God and with each other in Christ. It is to proclaim the Gospel, and promote justice, peace and love in the world. This is the teaching of the church's catechism, which goes on to say that the ministry of the *laos*, which means all people in Christ, is

> to represent Christ and his Church; to bear witness to him wherever they may be; and, according to the gifts given them, to carry on Christ's work of reconciliation in the world; and to take their place in the life, worship, and governance of the Church.

To do all of this is a tall order, but if one is asked how to develop a fuller spirituality, how to enter more and more deeply into communion with Christ, then one should point to all of these things. For to be in Christ is to be Christ's living presence in this twentieth century. Spirituality is not a matter of withdrawal from the world, but of participation in Christ's mission and ministry of sacrificial love and service in the world.

Spirituality is concerned with communion between the faithful Christian and Christ. The Christ with whom the Christian is in communion is the Son of God and Son of Man beyond all our partial images of him. Yet, as I have stated, if we are to enter into personal fellowship with Christ we must be able to regard the Christ as a person, and thus as someone whom we can "see." There is no one correct mental image of the Jesus of Nazareth

[133]

whom we worship as the Christ of faith. Depictions that are in keeping with those of the New Testament and tradition are adequate and forceful to the degree that they do in fact mediate Jesus Christ to us where we are, with our God-given abilities to perceive the truth and to detect falsehood. To a large extent, the man we "see" is related to our need or the needs of the world as we perceive them. In the twentieth century the human situation calls for prophetic vision and for compassion, for kindness and gentleness, for God's presence with those who suffer in this life. The Christ we worship is he who saves us from our own inhumanity and cares for us in our pain. In this age of nuclear threat we look with great intensity for the God of hope, the Christ who came and shall come, beyond our self-destruction and the earth's demise.

What we find between Christ and Christians, enabling the saving fellowship, is a current of communication, begun and enabled by the Holy Spirit. The Holy Spirit comes from God to open our eyes that we may "see" Jesus, who is present amongst us in word and sacrament. The Holy Spirit is active, too, inspiring the human response that we identify as prayer. Prayer, in the broadest sense, is our total response to God's saving activity in and through the Holy Spirit. Prayer is thus more than prayers; prayer is the Christian's life in relation to God. Prayer has to do with life-styles and with action as well as words. In the narrower sense, prayers are focal points or concentrates of our life in Christ, involved in the holy routine that informs and guides our lives.

Finally, the context in which the fellowship of Christ and the Christian occurs, through the activity of the Holy Spirit, through word and sacrament and the human response of prayer, is the holy community, the body of

Christ, of which Christ is the head and we are the members. To be in Christ is to be in the church and to be in the church is to be in Christ. We have explored some of the implications of this traditional understanding that has, in this twentieth century, radical implications. The further implications for all that we have been considering thus far, in terms of ourselves and the world in which we live, shall be our concern in the final chapter.

Spirituality and Society

The world in the twentieth century exists in a state of crisis. The crisis we face is global in character and involves both extreme danger and great opportunity. The threat of annihilation in a nuclear holocaust affects all of the world's societies; it conditions the outlooks of multitudes of individuals. The dread thought is that the time will come when some terrorist group will obtain access to nuclear warheads and, after holding this or that nation hostage for awhile, will trigger the holocaust. Such a threat, real or imagined, hangs over both conferences of world leaders and gatherings of families in remote places on the earth. In addition to the nuclear threat, and involved in its escalating proportions, there is the potentially disastrous competition among nations and multi-national corporations for the world's natural resources to support growing populations and expanding military and industrial demands. The situation is worsened as short-term cultivation of arable areas to supply much needed grains and other food commodities, turns fertile lands into deserts and dust-bowls, eroding the land and altering the environment in ways inhospitable to human habitation. The situation is one in which extreme poverty exists alongside extreme wealth, with debilitating effects upon both individuals and societies, and the creation of social environments characterized by mutual hostility rather than mutual caring and love.

We find verification for what we observe on a global scale in our own personal experience. Modern men and women are caught between a compulsive concern for self-identity and an insidious fear that if they dig too deeply, they will discover nothing of substance; perhaps *they* are the hollow men, the twittering inconsequential uncles and aunts. Self-doubts extend to interpersonal relationships, to family life, and to those intimate networks that begin and end with alarming rapidity. Doubts of self-worth and the reluctance to commit oneself to supposedly costly relationships erode interpersonal relationships. And so this society is characterized for many by loneliness and isolation in the midst of a constantly changing mass of humanity. In the macrocosm of global and national life, as well as the microcosm of personal and interpersonal existence, we are beset by the threat of annihilation — the dissolution of world and national order and of the consciousness-centered society — and by the fear of meaninglessness, of death, knowing that our passing is of little or no consequence to anyone, anywhere.

In the seventies, the Doctrine Commission of the Church of England, chaired by Hugh Montefiore, released a study of humanity in its relationship to nature that portrays our condition in a somewhat different way.

Moderns are presented as raising the right questions, while at the same time dismissing them, usually for real but inadequate reasons. For instance:

> The population of the world is exploding . . . Should we not do something about this? But why worry? If there is a disaster, it will strike the next generation and not ours . . . .

> We are using up non-renewable resources to the detriment of posterity. Should we not be doing something about this? But previous generations never worried about us. Science will find a way out of the difficulties . . . .

> We are endangering the future by a perilous and imprudent expansion of the production of energy from nuclear fission. Ought we not to abandon this? But man has always taken risks, regardless of the future. We must have energy or modern culture will collapse . . . .

As the report proceeds, its frame of reference becomes more personal.

> We are overburdening our minds and bodies by the increasing stress and tempo of life, with attendant stress illnesses. Ought we not to change our lifestyle? Yet statistically we are healthier than our forefathers . . . .

> We are dehumanizing life by the impersonal structures of modern society, by our addiction to socially destructive tools, by an obsession for consumer goods,

many of them useless, unnecessary and even un-
wanted. Ought we not to be putting the needs of
people and the cultivation of personal and communal
relations before our insatiable desire for things? But
mass-production methods are essential if goods are to
be produced for all, and why should goods be
produced unless the masses want them? If this is
what people want, then this is what they should
have.[52]

The crisis involves a wide spectrum of people in the developed countries and is effecting more and more in the
underdeveloped countries of the Third World. It includes
people who profess to be Christians, as well as people of
other religions and of no religion. Indeed, what H.
Richard Niebuhr called "culture Christianity" is dedicated
to confirming people in their most selfish and destructive
tendencies.

An extreme example, but one which is not altogether
out of keeping with much of American religion, concerns
the Reverend Terry Cole-Whitaker, the evangelist to the
"me" generation. As reported in the *Wall Street Journal*
of August 23, 1984, Terry Cole-Whitaker

is trim, tan and well-paid, just like the healthy-
looking Californians crowding into her religious ser-
vices. Her message, too, is one many of them can
identify with.

"You can have it all now!" she says excitedly.
"Being rich and happy doens't carry with it a burden
of guilt. If you are poor, you're irresponsible."

A lot of her parishioners are taking no chances of
that, to judge by their designer outfits and sleek cars.
And as they drive off in those Mercedes-Benzes and

Datsun 280Zs, many flash the bumper sticker their spiritual guide supplies: "Prosperity is your divine right."

The Rev. Terry is the evangelist of the yuppies. Bubbly, bouncy and relentlessly upbeat, she preaches a gospel of "happiness now" . . . Wealth is good . . . Money is only an energy flow. Live fully in the moment and create a heaven on earth. "We are the cause of our own happiness," she says.

When Christianity becomes a means of authenticating society's lusts and its avoidance of the crises it faces, Christianity becomes a part of the problem. The spirituality of such "culture Christianity" is a spirituality of blindness and dumbness dedicated to success in worldly terms and pleasure in its most hedonistic sense.

Such Christianity is not limited to the Terry Cole-Whitakers of this world. It is to be found in virtually every edifice identified as a "church," even among those who love to hear the choir sing the "Magnificat" according to the rules of Anglican chant. It is to be doubted that they even hear or understand its words:

He has shown strength with his arm,
He has scattered the proud in the imagination of
   their hearts,
he has put down the mighty from their thrones,
   and exalted those of low degree;
he has filled the hungry with good things,
and the rich he has sent empty away.

Nor can it be imagined how yuppie Christians explain away the testimony of the Beatitudes: "Blessed are you poor, for yours is the kingdom of God."

The more one thinks about it, the greater the dimensions of the present world crisis appear to be. What is to be done? One way of answering this question is to say that we need a spirituality which is suited to life in the present crisis. This answer is suggested by the work of an international society of scientists and other professionals founded by the Italian industrialist, Aurelio Peccei. The society is called the Club of Rome and it is concerned with the well-being of the world as a whole. The organization "is future-oriented in its thinking and must necessarily take into account the incongruities of the human condition, its values and goals, both actual and desireable, if the species is to survive."[53]

The second report to the Club of Rome, *Mankind at the Turning Point* (1974), considered the world crisis and urgently recommended a dramatic revolution in human values. It urged the development of world-consciousness, whereby individuals would come to identify themselves more with global society than with competing national units. Other aspects of this revolution in values would be a new ethic, according to which we would achieve greater satisfaction from saving and conserving resources than from spending and wasting them, and toward nature, a new attitude through which we would seek not the conquest of nature, but cooperation with nature, viewing ourselves as parts of nature. Above all, the report urged development of concern for future generations, concern that would enable people to surrender present luxuries so that future generations may be assured of sufficient resources to sustain life.[54]

These suggestions were not advanced in behalf of the Christian gospel. They were urged out of concern for the well-being of the human race now and in the future. Furthermore, it was the conviction of many of the participants in the studies leading up to the reports that the revolution in human values described in *Mankind at the Turning Point* would positively enhance life, and not turn it into a grim, ascetical, bare existence. The focus of this new ethic was upon quality of life, not quantity of possessions, upon mutual interests and concerns in the global village, and not upon bitter competition for world resources. In a sense these scientists and other professionals, some of whom were admittedly Christians, understood the true nature of Christian asceticism according to the great monastic rules. St. Benedict of Nursia admitted that in his rule he required some things that seemed too austere, but he believed that "as we advance in the practices of religion and faith, the heart insensibly opens and enlarges through the wonderful sweetness of his love, and we run in the way of God's commandments."[55]

Christians justly conclude that such values as those recommended by the report, *Mankind at the Turning Point*, are to be found in the Holy Scriptures and have been taught in the church through the centuries. From the beginning the Christian gospel has been for all people, although this was clearer to Paul than to Peter. Nationalism is contrary to Christianity and its commitment to a world-wide mission. Therefore consciousness of the world through which individuals come to identify themselves with global society rather than with competing national units should come naturally to Christians and should constitute an important element in their spirituality. That it does not come naturally testifies both to the way in which moderns identify their roots with the national units to which they belong and also to the way in which nationalism has come to dominate western thinking since the Peace of Westphalia in 1648.

The suggestion that there needs to be a new ethic –

distinct from the present ethic of a consumption-oriented society - whereby humans achieve greater satisfaction from saving and conserving resources than from spending and wasting them is compatible with the New Testament. Think of those injunctions that Christians be concerned for the poor, for those who hunger, and not engage in gluttony and waste. But chiefly we find there the example of Jesus, whose life was dedicated to sacrificial service on behalf of those in need, and not to the pursuit of power and wealth, the lusts of gentile kings. Furthermore, in Matthew 6, Jesus speaks of the necessity of serving God and not Mammon ("money," NEB), and of not being anxious about food or clothing. The fundamental need is to worship God; then all of these things, the food and the clothing needed both to sustain life and to serve God, will be added. In the Lord's Prayer there is the petition, "Give us this day our daily bread," which means, as Lancelot Andrewes pointed out, sufficient food for living, not groaning boards of food such as gluttons dream about. Christianity is concerned for that moderation urged upon us by the second report to the Club of Rome.

The suggestion that people seek not the conquest of nature, but cooperation with nature, agrees with Paul's words in Romans 8. There nature ("creation") is viewed as sharing in the stress, anxiety and pain that human beings feel, waiting with the whole of nature for redemption. Though Genesis refers to God's granting of power over nature in order to dominate and exploit it, these references are tempered and qualified by the concept of stewardship that also runs through the Scriptures. The great need for the development of concern for future generations, concern that will cause people to surrender present luxuries in order that future generations may have sufficient resources for life, is expressed in the Old and New Testaments in many ways. Most significantly, Jesus insists upon service (*diakonia*), which is intended to benefit the deprived in our world, but also looks toward the future and toward those who succeed the present disciples. This sense of responsibility for future generations has grown through the years and is expressed in Christian writings pertaining to parenthood and family life.

Another report to the Club of Rome, entitled *Goals for Mankind* (1977), emphasized two characteristics of Christianity: its universal character, for it is and always has been essentially global, and its strong ethical emphasis. Christianity has staying power, so the report says, "as a universal religion, relevant to all men without distinction of nation, race, or caste." Christianity possesses a strong ethic, such an ethic as is needed for the future:

> To be at one with God is to have the mind of Christ, who went about doing good. The marks of the Kingdom of God are justice and mercy, forgiveness, sharing, self-sacrifice on behalf of all who are in physical or spiritual need, and brotherhood with no distinctions of class or race. "By this shall all men know that ye are my disciples, if ye have love to one another."[56]

Christians As Change Agents

To live in Christ by the fellowship and activity of the Holy Spirit is to be in tune with the world, society and nature, renouncing the pressures exerted upon us, from within and without ourselves, to exploit society and nature in order to satiate our inordinate greeds. It is to live by the law of sacrifice and not by the self's love of self to the exclusion of others. Furthermore, to live in Christ is to be an agent of change, an instrument for the promulgation of a "new" ethic and an age-old spirituality.

In their book *Living in the Spirit*, Alan Jones and Rachel Hosmer write of the challenge we face as the world's resources approach their limits. We react to this painful thought in various ways. These authors mention denial and three forms that denial can take. One is to be overwhelmed by the painfulness of the challenge and to turn our attentions elsewhere. Another is to push on with business as usual. And the third:

> is to retreat to the *spiritual*, that is to say, to the spiritual understood as unworldly, subjective, and *religious*. When we cut off part of our life, that part which is reserved for worship, meditation, and personal development, from the life of the world and of society around us, and call it *spiritual*, we are denying the basic proclamation of Christianity, namely, that "the Word became flesh and dwelt among us."[57]

True Christian spirituality concerns life in the world, in the midst of the present global crisis. Jones and Hosmer admit that this spirituality, the spirituality of the Incarnate who was crucified, is not easy, nor is it pleasant. To follow Christ now is "to accept the pain and humiliation of having to reduce our standard of living so that all may share in the limited resources of the world, and to find in that acceptance a transforming gift, the seed of a new society." Hosmer and Jones go on to say:

The pattern of that society has already been given in the description in the Acts of the Apostles, the description of the church in Jerusalem, as a community that devoted itself to the teaching and fellowship of the Apostles, to the breaking of bread and of prayers, and to the community of goods.[58]

It is this society that Christianity cultivates.

It is true that, given the complexities of life in this twentieth century, it is rarely possible to recreate that simple communal life to which the testimony in Acts refers. Reading Paul's epistles and the rest of the Acts of the Apostles, one is led to question whether the example of the church of Jerusalem was ever followed, at least for very long. The religious orders that were founded in the time of the early church were, in part, protests against the laxity, worldliness and gluttony found in the church of that era. As protests they were reformist, seeking to recover the simplicity and purity of life as lived in the first church, the church of the apostles in Jerusalem. But in time the religious orders themselves stood in need of reform, having grown wealthy, lax, and gluttonous. Reform has continued as a major theme in the church's history. Time and time again attempts have been made to recover the original necessary experience. And this has been as it should be, given the condition of life in the world as we know it. When we look at it this way, what is essential is not so much an imitation of what little we know about the first Jerusalem church as an imitation of the spirit of that church, which was the Spirit of its Lord, the Spirit of sacrificial love and service. That Spirit expresses itself when someone in possession of a loaf of bread, seeing someone else in hunger, sets out to share not what is theirs alone, but what belongs to all, especially to those who hunger and are in need.

Christians are "change agents" first and foremost as they live their lives in Christ through the activity of the Holy Spirit, emulating in all that they say and do that sacrificial love and service which Christ displayed to those he met, especially to all who met him and continue to meet him at the cross. They live their lives in the spirit of humility, with contrition, recognizing their violations of the way of the cross, their backsliding, their yielding to temptations to indulge voracious appetites and to seek for self-satisfaction through the denial of the needs and wants of others. Christians are realists who know that they must seek the forgiveness of God and of others, and further newness of life. As they live through witnessing to God's abundant care and mercy, they are change agents. Their very lives stand in judgment against the destructive ways of those who live for the sake of self and of the self's idols in this world.

There is more to being change agents than this, however. Living in Christ, Christians are called to be agents of their Lord, feeding the hungry, giving drink to those who thirst, welcoming the stranger, clothing the naked, visiting the sick and those who are in prison. Yet this list from Matthew 25 is not exhaustive. Again, we are expected to view the needs of the world broadly, in accordance with the dedication that disciples have to sacrificial love and service. Furthermore, each group of those in need is to be regarded as widely as possible. Thus, to feed the hungry is not only to feed those who are physically hungry, but those who are spiritually hungry, those in need of the bread of life and the water of life. Most vitally it means that we not only send food to alleviate the hunger of those who are starving, but also work — calling upon all the resources at our command —

to assist them in the development of their own capacity to produce needed food-stuffs. In the same way, providing drink for those who thirst involves working to see that people have access to clean, non-polluted water. Again, clothing the naked also involves concern for adequate housing, which is our protection against the elements, just as our clothes are, and can be seen in terms of our need to "put on Christ" and to be "temples [houses] of the Holy Spirit." Welcoming strangers includes caring for all who are lonely in our midst, whatever the condition of their loneliness. Visiting the sick includes providing adequate health care for all people. Visiting those who are in prison also means providing the means for the re-habilitation of the incarcerated. In a word, Christian spirituality involves social service. It finds expression in the words and deeds of love of those who live in Christ, in communion, in union with him, words and deeds of sacrificial love and service extended to any and to all who are in need.

Prayer and Change

The change in attitudes necessitated by the world crisis points to the Christian concept of *metanoia*, a New Testament term for a change of mind and heart — repentance. *Metanoia*, turning or returning, is at the heart of Christian spirituality. It is the work of the Holy Spirit, the Spirit of God working with our spirits to bring about communion with God in Christ and with one another as we find ourselves in Christ.

In *True Prayer*, Kenneth Leech speaks of true spirituality as something quite different from the leisure-time activity it seems to be for many people. True spirituality concerns our everyday attitudes and activities in relation to all that confronts us. It also involves such an ethic, personal and social, as we have been considering. *Metanoia* is involved in Leech's statement that "discipleship involves a real transformation of character."[59] The fruits of that transformation demonstrate the close linkage between spirituality and ethics. The prophet Ezekiel describes the righteous person this way: "He opposes no man, he returns the debtor's pledge, he never robs. He gives bread to the hungry, and clothes to those who have none. He never lends either at discount or at interest. He shuns injustice and deals fairly between man and man" (Ezek. 18:16-17). Jeremiah 22:16 suggests that it is through dispensing justice to the poor and needy that the knowledge of God is discovered. The New Testament echoes the Old; see the Johannine statement that it is not possible to love God whom we have not seen if we love not the brother we have seen. Prayer, which is our union, our communion with God, occurs in the midst of human life. Prayer involves *metanoia*, change, with concrete results, results which are sometimes disturbing. To pray for the poor is to be engaged at the point where we live in alleviating the sufferings of the needy ones around us. To work for justice in the midst of injustice, in conscious cooperation with God, is to be engaged in the life of prayer. For as we serve the needs of others we engage in passionate, compassionate, responsible, thankful thought which we can identity as prayer.

Such prayer is not a simple matter. Leech puts it this way: "The pursuit of a prayerful life of simple love and discipleship sets us in isolation from and opposition to the mainstream, mammon-directed culture in which we live. We become deserters of technocracy, disaffiliating ourselves from its power, rejecting its false values. To pray is to drop out in the most profound and positive sense."[60] But only when viewed within the dominant society is such a life negative. There is a positive side from which to view "a prayer life of simple love and discipleship."

William Temple, long before he was Archbishop of Canterbury, but at a time when he was making his mark as a learned theologian and popular apologist for the faith, wrote of prayer, especially intercessory prayer, in this way:

> Prayer is an expression of love. Where there is no love, there cannot be any prayer. Sometimes the love may be very feeble, and only just strong enough to give rise to a real prayer; yet, if we make that prayer, it will strengthen the love it springs from, as any expression of an emotion tends to strengthen that emotion. And so a better prayer becomes possible. Prayer and love deepen each other. If we are Christians in any living sense, our love is sure to find expression in prayer, and so become deeper. Prayer, therefore, and especially mutual intercession, is one great means of increasing the volume of love in the world.[61]

This is not to say that prayer concerns only what happens to the praying person. It is a part of Christian faith to believe that God hears our prayer and that prayer contributes toward the ways in which God acts, although perhaps in ways that we do not expect. God hears our prayer and fulfills our petitions "as may be most expedient for us." But having said that, it must be affirmed that prayer has its positive effects upon the person who prays. To pray with all one's heart and mind and soul for all of those people known to us who are in danger or in any need, and to pray for things to happen or not to happen, keeping a disciplined and orderly intercessions list in the mind or in a book is one way of growing spiritually and of initiating action of benefit to others.

There may seem to be something too sparse and mechanical in the way in which Lancelot Andrewes listed matters for prayer in his *Private Devotions*, as when he asked God to be mindful of "Infants, Children, Lads, Youth, Men, Aged, The Hungry, Thirsty, Naked, Sick, Prisoners, Strangers, Harbourless, Unburied." In his devotions for Monday, Andrewes began his intercessions begging of the Lord,

> For all creatures,
>   the gift of
>   Healthful
>   Fruitful   times
>   Peaceful
> For all mankind,   Atheists, Ungodly,
>   Not Christians,   Heathens,
>   Turks, Jews,
>   Conversion;
> Christians,   Infirmities,
>   labouring under
>   Sins,
>   Restoration . . .
> Help and comfort to all men and women
>   labouring under
>   Dejection of mind,
>   Infirmity of body,
>   Poverty, trouble . . .

It was in his Monday devotions that he prayed

> For the Church
> Catholic,
>> confirmation, and
>> enlargement;
> Eastern,
>> deliverance, and
>> unity;
> Western,
>> perfection, and
>> peace;
> British,
>> supply of what is wanting,
>> establishment of what
>> remains . . .[62]

One must understand that Bishop Andrewes did not "rattle off" these prayers as we have them here. Each brief, terse reference on any given day could open into a vast area of concern in relation to specific persons or events. In the course of such devotions, Andrewes would find his own spirituality enlarged and he might find his day's work formed, at least in part, by his prayers. The volume of love would be increased within him and through him in the world about him.

It is perhaps simpler to understand this when looking at personal devotions, such as those of Lancelot Andrewes, but it is also true that the "Prayer for the whole state of Christ's Church," the "Prayers of the People," and other such corporate intercessions are means of enlarging love in those who pray. Through them, the volume of love in the world increases. The Prayers of the People in the Prayer Book begins with this direction:

[153]

> Prayer is opened with intercession for
> The Universal Church, its members, and its mission
> The Nation and all in authority
> The welfare of the world
> The concerns of the local community
> Those who suffer and those in any trouble
> The departed

The six forms that follow these directions help to add detail and substance to the outline; the people may add, in silence or aloud, their own more particular petitions. In the course of such petitions it may be expected that the people will find their own thoughts directed toward the needs of others, and thus be prepared through their prayer in church for prayer in deeds and words of love wherever they may be in the world.

William Temple contended that "prayer, especially intercessory prayer, is an expression of love on the part of him who prays towards those for whom he prays; for the Christian it is a natural and almost necessary expression of that love; and by expressing love it increases it." His further thought is that

> God is love; and the love from which prayer springs is the Holy Ghost at work in our hearts. The Christian can never think of love as a mere sentiment or state of feeling; it is a power; it is the supreme power of the world. That it should be generally realised as this is the first condition of human welfare. And one way to this is prayer, which expresses and so increases the love that is to prevail over all other forces.[63]

Prayer is therefore a means for effecting change in our society and in the world. Prayer is not irrelevant to social change and social well-being, but constitutes one means by which God working through the Holy Spirit ushers in his kingdom.

The Book of Common Prayer and Change

The *Book of Common Prayer* was conceived by Thomas Cranmer to be one of the chief instruments for overcoming the dominance of avarice and greed in sixteenth-century England, and of promoting and perfecting communion, community, and the common weal, or welfare. The first portion of it to be published in the reign of King Edward VI was *The Order of Communion* (1548). The *Order* was necessitated by a parliamentary act "against Revilers, and for Receiving Communion in Both Kinds," promulgated in 1547. The Act was a uniformity measure. It provided warning against those who reviled the Holy Communion, then more commonly known as the Mass, argued for the necessity of concord, and expressed the desire that the king's subjects should "study, rather for love than for fear" to do their duties, first to Almighty God, and then to his highness and the commonwealth, nourishing concord and love amongst all of the peoples. In ordering Holy Communion in both kinds, both bread and wine, and providing for the *Order of Communion* in English to be inserted into the Latin Mass, the Act placed considerable emphasis on communion, both the act of receiving consecrated bread and wine, and the concept. The word "communion" was to be a key word, understood in terms of *koinonia*, or table fellowship, as in 1 Cor. 10:16, and in terms of *menō*, *menein*, meaning to abide in or be in union with, as in John 6:54, the source of one of Cranmer's basic themes, expressed by the words "he in us and we in him." Richard Hooker discussed this in terms of participation, mutual participation, between ourselves and Christ and amongst each other in the congregation of the faithful.

Read with this in mind, the essential meaning of *The Order of Communion* is quite clear. The sacrament is "the blessed sacrament of unity," the instrument of God for the creation of the godly commonwealth, the community of mutual, sacrificial love and service. Thus the exhortations stress the necessity of partaking of the sacrament, while at the same time they urge preparation for this reception, a preparation that includes an act of reconciliation. The Invitation to Confession rings the changes on this: "You that do truly and earnestly repent you of your sins and offences committed to Almighty God, and be in love and charity with your neighbors, and intend to lead a new life . . . draw near and take this holy Sacrament to your comfort, make your humble confession to almighty God, and to his holy church here gathered together in his name . . . ." The Confession, Absolution, and Comfortable Words come next, followed by the Prayer of Humble Access with its doctrine of mutual participation. Finally, there is the communion itself - now regarded as vital to the sacrament. Whereas for many people in the late medieval church the Mass centered upon the epiphany of God in the consecration of the bread and wine as body and blood of Christ, now the focus of the sacrament was moving instead to the communion of priest and people and the coming of God in the reception of the elements. The change in the bread and wine itself then began to give way to the change in the people, turning them from preoccupation with self to the adoration of

God in Christ and sacrificial love and service as disciples of the Servant Lord.

The first prayer books in English took shape, in a sense, around this *Order*. One might say that they further emphasized communion and the community of forgiven sinners, renewed time and time again, for service in the world. Indeed, there seems to have been a progressive development of the communion theme, with increasing concern for the preaching of the Word of God and the celebration of the Holy Communion, so that the avaricious and rebellious nobility and commoners alike might be brought to repentance and live in charity with one another. Viewed in this light, the second Prayer Book (1552) is no decline from an ideal, but is rather the closer approximation of the ideal of communion for the sake of the common good. The consecration prayer was broken up in such a way that the communion of the people could be inserted into the midst of the prayer that emphasized the rejection of transubstantiation and other such views of the sacrament. Thus it stressed conformity to a view, expressed by many English theologians in the sixteenth and seventeenth centuries, that the consecration is in the use, not in any magical transformation of the elements of bread and wine.

It is necessary, in order to understand the impact of this view, to visualize the Holy Communion being celebrated at a table in a parish church. The table was set in the midst of the people and the communicants stood around it, repenting of their sins before one another, after having heard the Gospel read and the Word preached, drawing near to participate in the vital act of communion, receiving the body and blood of Christ who died for the sins of the world, giving thanks and pledging their lives to sacrificial love and service. In hearing, receiving, and pledging, each person, no matter what station in life he or she occupied, was involved in the process whereby true mutuality in community was to be realized and the *communio Christiana* strengthened.

It is not surprising that Cranmer and others in the sixteenth century should have viewed the Holy Communion as a social act. The Lord's Supper was understood in that way in the early church, and it has certainly been understood as a social act in the twentieth century. In the second century A.D. Justin Martyr spoke of the offering of prayers and thanksgivings and alms at the Eucharist. The alms were to be distributed to provide aid "to the orphans and widows and such as are in want by reason of sickness or other cause; and to those also that are in prison, and to strangers from abroad, in fact to all that are in need."[64] Dom Gregory Dix describes how the communicants in the early church gave themselves in the offering under the forms of bread and wine. Individuals were united in the offering so that the church gave herself "to *become* the Body of Christ, the sacrament, in order that receiving again the symbol of herself now transformed and hallowed, she might be truly that which by nature she is, the Body of Christ, and each of her members, members of Christ."[65] As such the church is Christ in and to the world ministering to those in need. The social significance of the Eucharist is clear, as it is in the ancient *Didache*, with its emphasis on unity and reconciliation: "As this broken bread was scattered upon the hills, and was gathered together and made one, so let thy Church be gathered together into thy kingdom from the ends of the earth."[66]

In the twentieth century there have been those who have viewed the Eucharist as "the sacrament of shared resources and out-poured life." Kenneth Leech bemoans the misunderstanding and neglect of the sacrament's true meaning and its social impact.

> All our life in the world is meant to be eucharistic. And yet we share the Eucharist in an unsharing world, a world in which bread is not equally distributed in communion. In this non-eucharistic world, it is the top fifteen percent who use up the marvelous achievements of science and technology in order to indulge in a crude materialistic life-style which prevents communion and ravages the created order. We share this Eucharist in a world of waste. The sacrament is reserved for the sick and needy: the bread of the world is thrown away.[67]

The Eucharist should be recognized in our time as the sacrament of shared bread. Down through the ages, and especially apparent in the earliest church, the Eucharist has been characterized by *koinonia* (fellowship) and communion with God in Christ, extending to fellowship and communion with one another in this world day by day. The Eucharist has social consequences. It dramatically portrays for all of those with faith to see and understand that the restored world, the redeemed world, will be one in which all of earth's resources, including the grain from which bread is made and the grapes from which wine is made, are held in common and shared. The vision conforms better to a simple rite, one in which people encounter people, and the bread and wine are shared around a table. The magnificent and elaborate high masses of cathedral churches tend to obscure for most people the basic meaning. It is the bread that matters, the shared bread, and what that means concerning the people involved in the sharing. It is the people who matter, those who offer the bread and receive it back transformed for their strengthening, that as forgiven sinners they may live sacrifically through loving and serving their brothers and sisters, to the glory of God and benefit of the neeedy.

This is how we should regard the *Book of Common Prayer* and the sacrament at its heart. It is a book that God uses by his Holy Spirit to change lives and to bring comfort to the suffering persons of this world, justice to those who are oppressed and judgment to those who ignore or oppose God's will. As such the Prayer Book is due honor and reverence, but for such merit it depends not on itself but on God who makes use of it and on the faithful who use it not for entertainment or creature comfort, but for the doing of God's will.

One more point must be made. Luke's account of the Last Supper is followed immediately by the narrative of the dispute that arose among Jesus' disciples concerning which of them was the greatest. Apparently it was while they were lingering after supper that Jesus said to them: "The kings of the Gentiles exercise lordship over them; and those in authority over them are called benefactors. But not so with you; rather let the greatest among you become as the youngest, and the leader as one who serves. For which is the greater, one who sits at table, or one who serves? Is it not the one who sits at table? But I am among you as one who serves" (Lk. 22:25-27). Should not *diakoneo* (service) in this passage be a key to understanding the end or purpose not only of the sacrament but of spirituality, and of life itself? In telling the disciples to serve, Jesus was creating a revolution. The aim of life for Greeks and Hebrews in the first century was greatness, such greatness and power and wealth as the "kings of the Gentiles" knew. Jesus, their king, sat at table with his followers and served them, an action which they evidently did not adequately perceive; he modeled for them, as he would far more dramatically upon the cross, the nature of true greatness. The Eucharist is the sacrament wherein we are served by the Lord God and are empowered by his Spirit to be servants of others, striving to meet the needs of others through sacrificial love and service.

Kenneth Leech draws attention to John's special and different account of the day on which the Last Supper occurred. In that account service is stressed in the story of the foot-washing (John 13:1-15). But, Leech says,

> the foot-washing becomes a meaningless ritual unless we take seriously the command of Jesus to 'wash one another's feet'. If Christian worship had revolved around foot-washing instead of bread-sharing, it is intriguing and depressing to think that now we would be involved in theological disputes about whether the feet should be sprinkled or totally immersed, whether the right or left feet should come first, who was authorized to wash feet, whether women's feet could be washed, and, even more serious, whether women could wash feet! In theological disputes about the Eucharist, we are in danger of forgetting that the Eucharist is meant to apply outside the church walls, just as foot-washing is.[68]

If spirituality is to be what it is meant to be, life lived in communion with God and with one another in Christ, life dedicated to Christ's mission and ministry of sacrificial love and service, then we must be able to perceive and understand the Eucharist for what it is: the sacrament of shared bread and shared lives. The irony is that much of the devotion paid to the Eucharist, and through the Eucharist to God, is hampered by petty concerns and misdirected thoughts, by misconceptions and squabbles over *adiaphora*, non-essentials.

Hope for the Future

We return at the end to the place where we began: the world in crisis and the need for a new life-style. Hope for the future in this world, with all that threatens its continuance, is based in large part on the change in attitudes and values that we can observe already. This change is largely the result of a realistic assessment, in the press, on television, and in the legislatures, of the present world-situation. Such realism arouses fear; if it does not provoke paralysis or escape, then it can stimulate positive action of one form or another. As the Doctrine Commission of the Church of England states in its report, however, we need much more: "Society as a whole will only adopt a different style of living if it has come under the impulse of a popular and imaginative way of seeing things in their wholeness." Such a vision comes through our understanding ourselves as creatures who find our true being "in a relationship of love with God and in co-operation with God in his purposes for the world." Such a relationship issues in action. We are led to see ourselves "and then to act as God's stewards or trustees in the created order, so far as we know it."[69] That is to say, we need the vision, attitudes and values that proceed from Christian spirituality, from that relationship with God and with others in God wherein the Holy Spirit, the "go-between God," cultivates sacrificial love that frees us from selfish preoccupation.

The Doctrine Commission suggests a way of stating the vision, attitudes and values inherent in Christian spirituality in relation to the global crisis. They do so in a creedal or confessional form that might very well find a place in Christian worship and be the basis for meditation by the faithful. This is the major part of it:

To accept God as Creator of all things implies that man's own creative activity should be in co-operation with the purposes of the Creator who has made all things good.

To accept man's sinfulness is to recognize the limitation of human goals and the uncertainty of human achievement.

To accept God as Savior is to work out our own salvation in union with him, and so to do our part in restoring and recreating what by our folly and frailty we have defaced or destroyed, and in helping to come to birth those good possibilities of the creation that have not yet been realized.

To "renounce the world, the flesh, and the devil" is to turn from grasping and greed and to enjoy people and things for their own sakes and not because we possess them.

To accept the Christian doctrine of Resurrection is to persevere in spite of setback and disaster, to resist the temptation to slip into a mood of fatalistic resignation, to believe that success can be attained through failures and so to live in hope.

To accept God as the Sanctifier of all things implies a respect for all existence, which is upheld by his Spirit and instinct with his energy.

To accept our nature as created in God's image and likeness and as destined to grow toward him involves responsible use of those godlike powers over the natural environment which God has put into our hands.

To hold that God has created the world for a purpose gives man a worthy goal in life, and hope to lift up his heart and to strengthen his efforts.

To believe that man's true citizenship is in heaven and that his true destiny lies beyond space and time enables him both to be involved in this world and yet to have a measure of detachment from it that permits radical changes such as would scarcely be possible if all his hopes were centered on this world . . . .[70]

Such a vision, it must be emphasized, properly belongs to a people, a community of those who find strength to hope in and through common worship, especially in and through word and sacrament. It is in the believing community that individuals are sustained through periods of doubt and fear, times when there seems to be no hope. They know, and they acknowledge they know, that they are borne up by the faith of those around them.

There is a great deal of talk these days about the necessity of having spiritual directors, or "soul friends." Sometimes what is meant by spiritual directors is people with special skills in the development of spiritual forma-

tion or growth. The danger here is that we do not
adequately perceive and acknowledge that the primary
source of spiritual direction is in and through the
community where the Holy Spirit dwells and works, that
member of the Trinity who is *the* spiritual director.
Spiritual direction comes to us through the community:
its belief, its worship, its discipline, its life together.
Spiritual direction comes to us through word and sacrament, and through the care and love of people around us
who accept us as we are, fully aware of the blemishes and
faults that characterize our humanity. Spiritual direction
in the church is a mutual activity. Those are best able to
be of assistance to others who are themselves assisted by
others. Insofar as "soul friends" are concerned, such
friends could be anyone, including the person who does
not know that he or she is a soul friend to you.

Admittedly, there are times when we need some specific help concerning some block in the path to spiritual
growth. Rightly, then, we turn to a priest or to someone
else whom we believe can help us, and whom we can
trust to keep confidences. It is important to seek
direction from someone who has sufficient experience of
life to understand our difficulties, and who will be
sympathetic, yet can still speak the necessary word of
judgment or of censure. The danger is that these special
situations can obscure the fact that we are enabled to live
according to the Christian vision by means of our
participation in the body of Christ, the church. It is the
vehicle of the Holy Spirit, and is therefore our spiritual
friend who provides, through its common life of prayer
and meditation, worship and discipline, mutual care and
love, all that we need to sustain us against the forces that
would distract us from wholeness of life in Christ Jesus
and in his ministry and mission in the world, forces

within and without, but chiefly our own self-preoccupation.

William Temple was fully aware of the fact that there is a sense in which each one of us, as cherished individuals, must stand alone before God. God alone knows the secrets of our hearts. Yet Temple also knew that we could not survive as Christians without the fellowship that we have in Christ Jesus. He explored this in many ways, here in terms of adoration and communion:

> Adoration is the form of worship in which we come nearest to Heaven; and, as has been remarked, while Heaven has often been compared to the performance of music, it has always been to a chorus or an orchestra, never to a solo. Each must render his own part, no doubt, or the full harmony suffers; but his part is a poor thing by itself. It is only the Church, the fellowship of the redeemed, that can offer worthy praise; and this will only be all that it aspires to be when the Church embraces all men. My praise will not be what it aspires to be until it is offered in concert with that of Indians and Chinese, of negroes and half-castes. All are wanted to make the harmony complete.[71]

The culmination of this unity is in the Eucharist where we find unity with Christ and with one another in him.

Spirituality is communion — with God in Christ and with one another in Christ. It is communion that respects, even honors, our individuality, but it is nevertheless communal. It is in communion that we discover our true identity as individuals. Therefore we are never altogether whole until we belong incidentally but intentionally to the fellowship, acknowledging that we become fully human, that which God created us to be, only through our identity with that fellowship which is ours in the body of Christ. But our belonging is never mindless; it is critical in the sense that we are alive to the possibilities for evil that exist in any group, and to the necessity of testing the spirits. We live, thus, in a dynamic relationship to the fellowship that provides us with hope. We live, that is, between the times, as pilgrims on our way to paradise, but not yet there. We participate in the fellowship which gives us a foretaste of that perfection which is to be in the fellowship of the saints that gather around the throne of God. Spirituality is communion and spirituality is, therefore, hope, for our spiritual journeys lead to the messianic table around which we shall gather with the blessed company of angels to sing praises to God, Father, Son, and Holy Spirit, the *alpha* and the *omega* of all that was, that is, that shall be.

> Worthy art thou, our Lord and God,
> to receive glory and honor and power,
> for thou didst create all things,
> and by thy will they existed and were created.

Notes

[1] Edwin Brock, *Invisibility is the Art of Survival* (New York: New Directions, 1972), p. 28.

[2] Paul Tillich, *Systematic Theology*, I (Chicago: The University of Chicago, 1951), pp. 174-178.

[3] Martin Marty, "Religion in America Since Mid-Century," *Daedalus*, 3/1, p. 155.

[4] James Oliver Robertson, *American Myth, American Reality* (New York: Hill and Wang, 1980), pp. 215-216.

[5] Quoted in Alan Jones, "New Vision for the Episcopate?" in *Theology*, 81 (July, 1978), p. 286.

[6] David Bohm, *Wholeness and the Implicate Order* (London, Boston, and Henley: Routledge and Kegan Paul, 1981), p. 3.

[7] R. L. Brett, "Mysticism and Incarnation in *Four Quartets*," *English* 16: 98-99.

[8] Andrew Louth, *Discerning the Mystery: An Essay on the Nature of Theology* (Oxford: Clarendon Press, 1983), pp. 1-4.

[9] Gordon S. Wakefield, ed., *The Westminster Dictionary of Spirituality* (Philadelphia: The Westminster Press, 1983), for the definition under "Spirituality" by the editor, pp. 361-362.

[10] Joe McCown, *Availability: Gabriel Marcel and the Phenomenology of Openness* (Missoula, Montana: Scholars

Press for The American Academy of Religion, n.d.), pp. 18-20.

[11] John V. Taylor, *The Go-Between God: The Holy Spirit and Christian Mission* (Philadelphia: Fortress Press, 1973), pp. 17-20, 91-93.

[12] Raymond G. Brown, *The Gospel According to John* (i-xii), The Anchor Bible (Garden City: Doubleday, 1966), p. 79.

[13] Karl Barth, *Church Dogmatics*, IV/2 (Edinburgh: T. & T. Clark, 1960), pp. 536-537.

[14] John B. Skinner, *The Christian Disciple* (Lanham, New York, London: University Press of America, 1984), p. 53.

[15] Harvey H. Guthrie, "Anglican Spirtuality: An Ethos and Some Issues," *Anglican Spirituality*, ed. W. J. Wolf (Wilton, Conn.: Morehouse-Barlow, 1982), p. 4.

[16] George Herbert, *The Latin Poetry of George Herbert*, trans. Mark McCloskey and Paul R. Murphy (Athens, Ohio), p. 84.

[17] John Jewel, *Works*, John Ayre, ed., Parker Society (Cambridge: University Press, 1847), 2:1123-1124.

[18] Lancelot Andrewes, *Ninety-Six Sermons*, Library of Anglo-Catholic Theology (Oxford, 1841), 2:134.

[19] See Joseph Hall, *Works*, Josiah Pratt, ed., 10 vols. (London, 1808), 7:43-73, for *The Art of Divine Meditation*. See my article: "Joseph Hall, *The Art of Divine Meditation*, and Anglican Spirituality," in *The Roots of the Modern Christian Tradition*, The Spirituality of Western Christendom, II, Rozanne E. Elder, ed. (Kalamazoo:

Cistercian Publications, 1984), pp. 200-228.

[20] Thomas Wilson, *The Art of Rhetoric, for the use of all such as are studious of Eloquence* (London, 1553), fol. 71v.

[21] Andrewes, *Ninety-Six Sermons*, 2:137.

[22] Helen Gardner, *The Divine Poems of John Donne* (Oxford: The Clarendon Press, 1978), espec. pp. 1-1v.

[23] Stephen Sykes, *The Identity of Christianity* (London: S.P.C.K., 1984), p. 275.

[24] Jacob Epstein *Epstein: an Autobiography*, 2nd ed. (London: Vista Books, 1963), p. 99.

[25] Ibid., p. 102.

[26] Horton Davies, *Worship and Theology in England*, Vol. 3 (Princeton, N.J.: Princeton University Press, 1965), pp. 98-99.

[27] Horton Davies and Hugh Davies, *Sacred Art in a Secular Century* (Collegeville, Minn.: The Liturgical Press, 1978), pp. 66-67.

[28] Ibid., p. 32.

[29] Epstein, *Autobiography*, p. 259.

[30] Ibid., p. 262.

[31] Walker Percy, *The Moviegoer* (New York: Avon, 1980), pp. 53, 226.

[32] William Barrett, *The Illusion of Technique* (Garden

City, N.Y.: Anchor Press/Doubleday, 1978), pp. 21-22.

[33] I am indebted to Hugh Davies and Sally Yard for "Images of Deluge and Apocalypse: The Recent Work of Robert Morris," in *The Divine Drama in History and Liturgy*, John E. Booty, ed. (Allison Park, Pa.: Pickwick Publications, 1984), pp. 3-20.

[34] Edwin Muir, *Collected Poems* (New York: Oxford University Press, 1976), pp. 223-224.

[35] W. H. Auden, *Collected Poems* (New York: Random House, 1945), p. 419.

[36] Taylor, p. 17.

[37] Ibid., p. 19.

[38] Ibid., p. 18.

[39] John Macquarrie, *Paths in Spirituality* (New York: Harper & Row, 1972), p. 30.

[40] Martin Thornton, *Prayer: A New Encounter* (New York: Morehouse-Barlow, 1972), p. 29.

[41] Taylor, p. 235.

[42] Kenneth Leech, *True Prayer: An Invitation to Christian Spirituality* (San Francisco: Harper & Row, 1980), p. 83.

[43] Ibid., p. 7.

[44] Julian of Norwich, *Showings*, Ed. and trans. Edmund Colledge and James Walsh (New York: Paulist Press, 1978), p. 254. This is in Chapter 43 of the long text.

[45] Henri de Lubac, *Catholicism* (London, 1950), p. 29.

[46] Karl Ludwig Schmidt, "The Church," p. 10, in J.R. Coates, ed., *Bible Key Words from Gerhard Kittel's Theologisches Wirterbuch zum Neuen Testament* (New York: Harper and Brothers, 1951).

[47] Ibid., p. 21.

[48] C. K. Barrett, *The Second Epistle to the Corinthians* (New York: Harper & Row, 1973), p. 199.

[49] Evelyn Underhill, *Worship* (New York: Harper and Brothers, 1937), p. 84.

[50] Ibid., p. 86.

[51] R. K. Orchard, *Missions in a Time of Testing* (London: Lutterworth Press, 1964), p. 197.

[52] *Man and Nature*, Hugh Montefiore, ed., The Doctrine Commission of the Church of England (London: Collins, 1975), pp. 73-75.

[53] Ervin Laszlo et al., *Goals for Mankind*, A Report to the Club of Rome on the New Horizons of Global Community (New York: E. P. Dutton, 1977), p. 7.

[54] Mihajlo Lesarovic and Eduard Pestel, *Mankind at the Turning Point*, The Second Report to the Club of Rome (New York: E. P. Dutton and Co., Inc. / Reader's Digest Press, 1974), p. 147.

[55] The Rule of St. Benedict, *Western Asceticism*, trans. Owen Chadwick, The Library of Christian Classics, Vol. 12 (Philadelphia: The Westminster Press, 1958), p. 293.

[56] Laszlo, *Goals for Mankind*, p. 375.

[57] Rachel Hosmer and Alan Jones, *Living in the Spirit*, (New York: Seabury, 1979), pp. 230-231.

[58] Ibid., p. 231.

[59] Leech, p. 79.

[60] Ibid., p. 81.

[61] William Temple, *Personal Religion and the Life of Fellowship* (London: Longmans, Green, 1926), pp. 39-40.

[62] See *The Private Devotions of Lancelot Andrewes*, ed. F. E. Brightman (New York: Living Age Books, 1961), pp. 59-60.

[63] Temple, p. 40.

[64] Justin Martyr, *First Apology*, ch. 67.

[65] Dom Gregory Dix, *The Shape of the Liturgy* (Westminster: Dacre Press, 1945), p. 117.

[66] *The Didache*, ch. 9.

[67] Leech, p. 110.

[68] Ibid., pp. 110-111.

[69] *Man and Nature*, p. 77.

[70] Ibid., pp. 77-78.

[71] Temple, p. 48.